MW00649545

Dear Cthulhu,

I'm five years old and I got a kitten for Christmas. It was the most wonderful little cat in the world. He would play with string and let me pet him all day long. I named him Buttons. One day a month ago, Buttons got out and we couldn't find him. It was a white, wintery day and my family had been making a snowman and we didn't see where Buttons went. We looked for weeks, even put up flyers and signs, but no Buttons. Then we got a warm day and the snow melted. We found Buttons dead on the lawn. We had a funeral and buried him.

After the funeral, my big sister whispered in my ear that the snowman we made had come to life and eaten Buttons, then pooped him out onto the lawn underneath the snow. I think she's making it up, especially since all the snowmen on the Christmas specials are happy, friendly, and don't eat pets. I've been having nightmares about snowman chasing me and trying to eat me as a herd of cats run by. They all have Buttons's face. I need to know the truth. Can snowman come alive and eat cats? Or kids? The weatherman is saying we're supposed to get a big blizzard this weekend. My parents are already talking about making another snowman. I need to know whether or not I have to stop them. Thank you.

– Five Years Old and Missing Buttons.

Dear Missing,

Most snowmen do not even have a chance of doing anything but melting. For a snowman to come to life, it requires dark magic far beyond what the average human could manage. However, there could be an evil sorcerer or witch in your neighborhood that is going around and bringing snowmen to life. And if that is the case, you are lucky all it ate was a kitten. One evil snowman broke into a family's house and devoured them all. He almost got away with it too but made the mistake of crossing in front of the fireplace and melted. All the police found was a carrot and two eyes made out of coal. I checked the weather report for your area and they are saying it is going to be good packing snow. I suggest putting the heat in your house up to ninety degrees and sleeping with an acetylene torch instead of a Teddy bear just in case. Oh, and don't go outside until at least springtime.

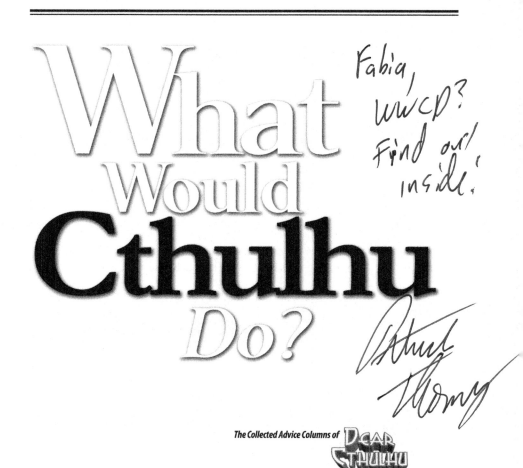

What Would Cthulhu Do?

Fabia,
WWCD?
Find out!
inside!

The Collected Advice Columns of Dear Cthulhu

Vol. 4

PATRICK THOMAS

PADWOLF
PUBLISHING

PADWOLF PUBLISHING INC.
WWW.PADWOLF.COM
www.facebook.com/Padwolf

WWW.PATTHOMAS.NET
www.facebook.com/PatrickThomasAuthor

WHAT WOULD CTHULHU DO?
The Collected Advice Columns of Dear Cthulhu Vol. 4

© 2016 Patrick Thomas

Many of the letters were previously published in Tales of the Talisman, Nth Degree, Dig This Real, and The Realm Beyond magazines.

Book edited by John L. French

Cover Art by Patrick Thomas and Roy Mauritsen

Cover Design by Roy Mauritsen

Dear Cthulhu is © & TM Patrick Thomas

10-digit ISBN 1-890096-68-7, 13 digit ISBN 978-1-890096-68-7
Printed in the USA
First Printing

If you have any additional questions that Cthulhu can answer, and Cthulhu can answer all questions, Dear Cthulhu welcomes letters and questions at DearCthulhu@dearcthulhu.com. All letters become the property of Dear Cthulhu and may be used in future columns. Sending financial offerings along with your questions is not necessary but is always appreciated.

Anyone foolish enough to follow Dear Cthulhu's advice does so at their own peril.

For Erin and Colin-
May I never give you bad advice.

Dear Cthulhu,

My wife is a witch. I don't mean it as an insult. She actually thinks she's a witch. I'm not talking one of these nice Wiccan witches that like to help the Earth and people and stuff. I'm talking an evil woman with magical powers. She's one that wants to cook children in the oven, which makes me glad for the first time that we don't have any kids.

"Witchy–poo" seemed normal enough when I married her. I know a lot of my buddies have gotten the seven-year itch, but for our last anniversary, I got the seven-year witch. Witchy-poo started dressing in tattered black dresses and wore a pointed hat. I'll admit I kind of settled when I got married, figuring she was the best that I was going to get. Our love life has never been all that exciting. I thought that had all changed one night when I got home from work. My wife met me at the door in her new black ensemble, the front of which was as low-cut as anything she's ever worn and had slits up both legs to her thighs. Then she demanded I take off my clothes and let her tie me down on our kitchen table. I did what she said as it was the most action I'd seen in years and it was our seventh anniversary. I thought she had been reading 50 Shades of Kinky or something and this was my present. Instead of her getting her fun freak on with me, she clipped a lock of my hair and my toenails then threw then into a bubbling pot on the stove. Next, she picked up a big steak knife and held it over my chest like she was going to cut my heart out. I think she would've done it too if the phone hadn't rung. It was the only time in my life that I was happy to get a call from a telemarketer.

I started rocking my body back and forth. Fortunately, we had a cheap dining set and I managed to break a leg off. The table fell over and I hit the floor but managed to get untied before my wife hung up the phone. My wife complained that I had ruined her sacrifice to her dark lord and waved some stick she'd probably gotten from the backyard at me. Then she told me she had turned me into a frog. I could see my naked self in the mirror. I wasn't green or small, but on some level, I was still hoping to get some, so I played along and hopped and ribbited. I guess I was hoping she would try to turn me back into a man by kissing me. When I tried for a smooch, she smacked me across the face and asked me to get back on the table so she could finish her sacrifice. I declined and locked myself in the guest room.

That was last week and I've been sleeping in said guest room with the door locked ever since. I'm not exactly sure what she's doing while I'm at work, but the shelves where she used to keep canned vegetables and jams seem to be filling up with jars filled with animal body parts.

I'm too embarrassed to go to the police. I make women's underwear at a factory and in my line of work a guy who can't handle his wife would be laughed at. I thought about divorcing her, but we don't have a prenup and she's been a housewife for the last seven years. She'll get half of everything I've worked for.

I'm pretty sure she doesn't have any real magic powers because she used the hair and nails she boiled to make a voodoo doll that she keeps poking with needles, most disturbingly in the groin area, but nothing's happened to me. I started cashing out some accounts so I can hide the money so she doesn't get it, but besides that what can I do to get rid of her? While I've never been really that in love with her, I still don't want to kill her. Especially since I doubt I'd get away with it. I'm hoping you'll have a better idea.

– Worried Husband of a Want-to-be Witch

Dear Worried,

Cthulhu is glad to see a human finally paying attention to some of Cthulhu's teachings. As I've said repeatedly, all of humanity will one day be Cthulhu's personal property. Humans should not kill other humans because you are damaging that which belongs to Cthulhu.

However, I am perturbed at your lack of conviction to your marriage vows. As longtime readers know, the Cult of Cthulhu is the twelfth fastest growing religion in the world. My worshipers all make vows of obedience to me. These vows are not unlike marriage vows, although obviously far more important. It troubles me whenever humans do not take the vows they make seriously because I do not want this lackadaisical attitude to infect those who have vowed their lives and souls in service to me. Where would Cthulhu be if my cultists decided they didn't have to do everything I commanded? I would be constantly having to discipline and police them. It is simply so much easier when they live in fear of me, too terrified to ever break a vow. Therefore, other humans should not be setting a poor example and breaking vows. Whether or not you love your wife does not enter into matters. You vowed to be together in sickness and in health and it is obvious that your wife is most likely in the throes of a mental illness. Instead of trying to figure out a way to get rid of her and sever your vows, you should be looking for a way to get her the mental health treatment she is in need of. In most states, a person who is a danger to themselves or others – she qualifies after having trying to sacrifice you to a dark lord who is not Cthulhu – can be committed against her will for psychiatric observation. The time for the commitment period varies, but if she is as bad as you say even a short observation would be enough for the doctors to realize she is mentally ill and perhaps come up with a way to treat her changing personality and delusions.

You claim to be too embarrassed to let others know that you cannot "handle" your wife. Your true embarrassment should lie with the fact that you are not looking out for her best interest as your marriage vows demand. Take care of your spouse and get her the help that she needs. And if she is looking to worship a dark deity, encourage her to do the smart thing and worship Cthulhu.

Dear Cthulhu,

My name is Nate and I have a teddy bear named Growler who is my best friend in the world. I'm eleven years old and my mom and dad say I'm too old to be sleeping with a stuffed animal and want me to get rid of him. They even tried to throw him out when I was at school but I got lucky. When I got off the bus, I saw the garbage men dumping our trash into their truck and caught a glimpse of Growler's arms. I chased the truck down the block and got my bear back. He smelled bad until I was able run him through the washing machine.

I told my mom and dad if they did that again I was going to run away. However, they still say I'm too old to be sleeping with a stuffed bear. I really don't see the problem. I'm an only child and I haven't brought Growler to school since I was in kindergarten so it really doesn't affect anything else I do. Maybe one day I won't want to cuddle with Growler at bedtime, but shouldn't that choice be up to me? Mom and Dad and I have agreed to abide by whatever you recommend. Thank you for your help.

-Nate and Growler

Dear Nate,

You are unusually wise for your young age in coming to Cthulhu for advice. Your parents are likely embarrassed by your sleeping with your stuffed bear. They feel that that is the act of a young child. The plus side is that they must view you as an older child or maybe even a young adult. They may be concerned that if they don't break you from the habit you might go away to college still sleeping with the bear and be made fun of. In days of old, the ribbing and teasing one could endure was limited to a small circle of acquaintances, but these days with the Internet, bullying and mockery can be seen by millions and last a lifetime. They likely are simply concerned for your well-being.

However, if you're not ready to give up the bear, it might be an upsetting and emotionally traumatic experience for you. There are several options available. Consider going to sleep with your bear and then after you are asleep having your parents come in and put the bear on a shelf where you could see him if you wake up. You could also get an extra pillowcase and hide Growler inside it where you would be able to still hold him and know he was there, while he would not be visible to others. Many adults sleep with what is called a body pillow, so you might consider getting one of those instead. Or you could continue doing exactly what you are doing, although you should work toward the day you would consider another person as your best friend instead of a toy. Cthulhu has gotten letters from others who never gave up their bear or stuffed animal. As they got older, some developed romantic and procreation feelings toward their long time stuffed friends. This never ends well for those letter writers, leaving them social outcasts and pariahs, so it might be best if you did make the effort before you get too much older to make a break from your bear. Just do it on your own schedule. Remember, do not allow others to force you to do something you do not want to do unless you are dealing with Cthulhu.

Dear Cthulhu,

I'm a new single mother and I'm slowly going insane. I feel as if any moment I might crack and go postal.

My son is five months old and hasn't slept for more than three hours since he was born. I'm exhausted. I can barely keep my eyes open at work, which is bad because I drive a school bus.

To compound everything, I am convinced I've got postpartum depression. I talked to my doctor about it. She gave me some medicine, but it hasn't helped. I'm barely able to function. I'm afraid to even take a sleeping pill to get one good night's sleep because I'm worried my son could die before I wake up. Of course, when he wakes me up after the only twenty minutes of sleep I've gotten in days, I worry that I might kill him myself.

I'm at the end of my rope. Please tell me what I should do.

– Haggard Mom from Hagerstown

Dear Haggard,

Get a babysitter long enough for you to sleep. If you cannot afford one, seek other solutions. You never mentioned anything about the sperm donor for your offspring – did he run off? Do you know who he is? If so, a simple paternity test can assure you of child support payments, which could be used to hire a sitter.

Do you have family or friends? Perhaps you could convince one of them to take your child for a night to give you a break and then take a sleep aid. A good night's rest will make things look much better. In fact, if you have many close friends, ask each of them to do this on a rotating basis. It should help you cope immensely.

If you are unlikeable and without any people who care about you, then perhaps consider giving the baby something to help him sleep. There are many children's medicines which would not harm the child, but have sleepiness is a side effect. Many of these are available over-the-counter. Although many humans would consider doing this bad parenting, *they* have probably slept in the last week.

Cthulhu may be stating the obvious here, but are you taking your infant to a pediatrician? There are various conditions and problems an infant may have that will cause them to have difficulty sleeping. Some of them are treatable. If you are lucky, your doctor might find a solution that would save your sanity as well as your family bond.

Of course, there is another option if you are simply looking for a way out of the mess your loins have gotten you into. Most states have a law that allows a mother who is in over her head to drop off a baby at a hospital or a fire or police station without fear of repercussions or being arrested for abandonment. There is also the possibility of giving the child up for adoption. There are many parents who are unable to conceive offspring of their own and are desperate for a chance to raise the unwanted offspring of another. In fact, Cthulhu himself would be more than happy to take this morsel… rather darling child off your hands. Cthulhu can personally guarantee that the child will never want for anything again. And then the two of you will be able to rest in peace, although perhaps in different ways.

Dear Cthulhu,

My husband "Spot" is a real dog. I don't mean then he runs around and cheats on me with other women. It's just that sometimes he seems to believe that he is actually a canine.

When we first got married, we had romantic candlelit dinners. Now he wants to eat out of a bowl on the floor. At first, it was a cute idiosyncrasy, but now it's affecting every aspect of our lives together. I'll be washing the dishes and suddenly he's humping my leg. Our sex life has gone down the toilet, which now he, of course, drinks out of. He only wants to make love in one position. I bet you won't have any trouble guessing which one.

Worse, when there are thunderstorms, he whimpers and hides under the bed, trembling and shaking. Between the bed vibrating and his crying, I can't get any sleep. It's affecting my job. Spot can telecommute because he's an accountant.

I've been suffering in silence. Who could I talk to about this? I've talked to Spot at great length. It hasn't done any good. And now he wants to take his behavior outside of the house. He bought a collar and leash. Spot wants me to take him for walks around our neighborhood. I told him no, especially after he explained that he bought me a pooper scooper to clean up after him.

I've thought about leaving him, but he makes twice as much as I do and even with alimony I'll never be able to afford a house as nice as the one we have. What can I do? It's driving me crazy.

– Married to a Deranged Doggie Dude in Denver.

Dear Married,

There are some advice givers who would recommend that you and your spouse immediately get counseling so you can be more accepting of him and he can change his behavior. However, this would take years, cost a small fortune and quite frankly, there is no guarantee that it will do either of you any good. Fortunately for you, Cthulhu is not one of those advice givers.

If Spot wants to act like a dog, treat him like one. The first thing you need to know about dog behavior is they understand dominance and submission. You need to immediately assert yourself as the dominant. He wants a collar and leash? Fine, get him one, but make sure it is a choker collar. Every time he does something you do not like, give it a tug. He makes a mess in the house, you rub his nose in it. He does not listen? You take a rolled up newspaper and smack him on the nose with it. Do this and in a week or two, Cthulhu practically guarantees either he will be obeying you perfectly or he will stop this behavior. Either way, you come out ahead.

If this doesn't work and he refuses to obey, simply tell him that if he doesn't shape up, you will take him and have him fixed. And they fix dogs differently than they fix men. They don't snip and leave the parts, they remove them completely. He may be delusional and think that he is a dog, but he is still a male dog. You shouldn't have any trouble after that. And if you do, show you mean business and have the procedure done. Unless you want to have his puppies first.

Dear Cthulhu,

I have quite a dilemma. Last week my wife and her identical twin sister were in a fatal automobile accident. It was a senseless tragedy. "Gemini" fancied herself an auto mechanic after watching a *Pimp My Pinto* marathon on TV. When the brakes on her car started to go, she decided to fix them herself. I tried to tell her that there shouldn't be any parts left over when she was done, especially the pads, but she wasn't having any of it.

As you might have guessed the brakes failed.

Also, her airbags didn't go off. She had fixed them the week before, even though they weren't broken. I argued with her that she needed a real air cartridge, not a can of whipped cream, but again she wouldn't listen. We had got a case of them from a warehouse club when she was going through a dairy kink phase and figured since they had compressed air it would work just as well. Ironically, she crashed into an ice cream truck, so the whipped cream didn't send off any red flags to the investigators.

The sisters had a double funeral and were laid out in identical dresses. I think they would've wanted it this way. They went to the same college so they could graduate together. My wife and I had to wait for years to get married until her sister "Gemina" found a guy so they could have a double wedding. Of course, we all had to go to the same honeymoon destination and have rooms next door to each other. Because they dressed alike, they often insisted that we husbands do the same. We even had to buy townhouses that shared a wall so the girls didn't have to be apart.

Gemini and I had a very active and fulfilling sex life. We were both what you would call sex addicts, but since we both had the affliction it worked out fantastically, sometimes having sex six or seven times in a day. The viewing was hard on me, especially with no bangie-bangie for a couple of days. It was particularly hard on one part of me if you get my drift. So after the wake, I snuck into the funeral home and broke into the cooler where they kept the bodies. I opened up my wife's coffin, removed her clothes from the waist down and gave her one great big final sendoff.

I hate to admit it, but it was fantastic. Gemini was a little bit dominant in bed and we always had to do what she wanted. This time, it was all about me.

I laid my head on her chest, like I did when she was still alive, and cuddled with her in the afterglow. Then before I got up, I reached out and pinched her left nipple. It was a tradition, something I did after we were done with sex. Then I would give her nipple ring a playful tug, only, this time, it wasn't there. My first thought was that the mortician had removed it and I was furious. Gemini loved her piercings – belly button, nipple, tongue, and uvula. Then a horrible idea crossed my mind and I reached out to feel her right breast. There was there was a nipple ring, but it was on the wrong side.

I had slept with her sister! In the 10 years Gemini and I were together, I never once cheated on her. I've never even touched another woman unless you count the 47 threesomes we were involved in. Knowing I had intercourse with someone besides her made me sick to my stomach. Part of me felt I needed to man up and go over and bang my dead wife anyway, but I was too ashamed. And the cooler was really cold if you know what I mean. But mainly I didn't want her to realize that I cheated on her with her own sister, so I straightened up Gemina and left the funeral home.

I cried all through the service. People thought it was because I missed my wife. That was true, but I was more upset about my screw-up. If Gemini was still alive, she'd kill me. Plus, what was supposed to be a beautiful, last sendoff turned into something cheap and tawdry.

Do you think what I did counted as adultery? Because I believe in God and I don't want to have to die and explain why I committed adultery or get kept out of heaven for it. Also, since the girls had to do everything together from the wedding to the honeymoon to even where we bought a home, I live next door to my brother-in-law and see him every day. I have trouble looking him in the eyes. He thinks it's from grief and keeps hugging me. I was wondering if I should confess and tell him I slept with his dead wife. I'm just not sure how he'd take it. What should I do?

     – NecroPhil

Dear NecroPhil,

     What you did could not be considered adultery. Wedding vows almost universally are valid only up until the death of one of the participants, although there is a tradition in China where men can marry ghost brides who are already dead. To my knowledge these unions are not consummated, unlike yours. What you did is necrophilia. Cthulhu finds it interesting that you're worried about what your God will think about you cheating on your dead wife with her dead sister and not let you into heaven for it, but you seem to have no qualms or worries about explaining why you had intercourse with a corpse. I think that would be the more likely sin to disqualify you from a pleasant afterlife.

     As for discussing your indiscretion with your brother-in-law, that depends on whether or not you yourself would like to join your wife in the hereafter. It has been Cthulhu's experience with human males that they are very protective of the women they procreate with, especially if they have taken marriage vows with the female in question. Were your brother-on-law to find out that you violated his deceased wife, he might send you to join her. I suggest remaining silent on the matter.

Dear Cthulhu,

My wife and I have been married six years and we've been trying for five of those to have a child. The love of my life has something called endometriosis, which makes it very hard, if not impossible, for her to conceive. We depleted our meager savings to try fertility treatments, all to no avail. A while back we came to the realization that we just weren't going to be able to have children of our own, so we started to look into adoption.

We'd like to adopt from this country, but our state has some stupid law that the mother of the child has a year to change her mind. I can't imagine the heartbreak if after 364 days the birth mother decided she'd changed her mind and wanted our baby back. It'd crush me and probably kill my poor wife. We've considered adopting from overseas, but I couldn't believe how expensive it is. We were looking at least fifty grand, sometimes more. We simply don't have that kind of money. We barely managed to scrape together five grand after six months of eating peanut butter sandwiches and Ramen noodles.

One way around needing most of the money was to find someone who wanted to give away their baby. Sadly, we're not the only ones trying this route. The pregnant young girls treat the situation like a reality show and pick the couples with the flashiest cars. We're not allowed to give them money, but I know for a fact that some of the couples who were chosen gave the girls expensive gifts.

I needed to get around the rich people who were blocking our plays, so I started trolling the seedier parts of town and talking to hookers. I told them if they ever got pregnant, not to have an abortion because my wife and I would be happy to adopt the child.

Next thing you know, I got arrested for prostitution in a sting operation. The girls told me they were working and had to be paid for their time. I wanted to get in their good graces, so I paid in case they got pregnant in the future.

The cops say the charges will stick because I gave the girls money, but all the girls insisted that I paid them just to talk to them. The cops don't believe them either because that story gets them off the hook too. I told anyone who would listen that I wasn't trying to have sex with anyone, I was just giving them an option of what to do should they ever get pregnant. Now the District Attorney's Office is talking about adding baby trafficking to my indictment.

My bail is ten grand, so I can't even get out. We don't have that much. I'm sitting in the slammer in a city two hours from home and running through all my vacation days. I've only told my wife that I'm trying to figure out a way to get us a child.

I am emailing this to you from jail. We get twenty minutes of computer time every day. I have a public defender I'm not sure graduated from law school in this country. He certainly doesn't act like he knows what he's doing. He told me he was going to try and see if he could plea bargain it down to endangerment of a minor, even though I explained to him there were no actual children involved.

At this point, I'm tempted to defend myself. What should I do?

– Paternally Perturbed Man in Modesto

Dear Perturbed,

Truthfully, Cthulhu has never understood the innate need of humans to produce offspring. The instinctual imperative does help to keep the species propagated, but let us continue to be truthful. Humans are so obsessed with procreation that even with birth control, there will be mistakes that happen and more children born.

Why just last month, Cthulhu got a letter from a woman with postpartum depression similar to the one above, whose screaming and crying infant was keeping her up at all hours of the night. It was driving her insane. Cthulhu offered her a win-win situation and Cthulhu adopted the child. She now has her life back and I had a wonderful child. You would not believe how plump and sweet the child was, but enough about my dinner and back to your issue.

There is a simple way to get yourself out of jail – simply plead guilty. Unless there is some sort of unusual bid for election to a higher office happening, prostitution stings usually involve a fine and a public shaming in the papers. Offer to plead guilty to the prostitution if they dropped the other charges, pay the few hundred dollar fine and go back home to your wife.

Then before continuing on this mad quest, Cthulhu suggests you take a closer look at the people around you who have small children and see how tired and unhappy they really are. Then look at those with teenagers, especially rebellious ones and see the heartache these offspring are causing their parents. If you look at this logically, you shall realize how much better off you are without children.

If this does not change your mind, simply inform your wife that you are going to try to have an affair with another woman. I know at first this will seem like something she would not want, but then explain to her that you're only doing it to get the woman pregnant. Then after the child is born, you can sue for shared custody and your wife can help you raise your illegitimate offspring. Admittedly, the best you could hope for to have the child half the time, but is not half a child better than none? Especially if served with a good hollandaise sauce.

Dear Cthulhu,

My mother is ruining my life with her controlling ways. I don't mean a little bit controlling. She wants to micromanage every aspect of my life – what I wear, what I do, and who my friends are to what I eat and what soap I shower with. It's driving me nuts. I'm beginning to think she never wants me to leave home. I'd like to go out on my own someday and find a woman to marry. Most of my other friends' mothers were obsessed with them having kids so they can have grandchildren. My mother doesn't seem to care about that.

It's really getting to me. Part of me is beginning to wonder if it's too late for me to make my way in the world. My birthday is next week and I'll be seventy-six.

This all started back when I was seventeen. In fact, it was the night of my senior prom. I had a date with Mildred Dunn, the prettiest girl in the whole school who'd actually go out with me. My dad had died earlier that year in a freak dam accident. He was drinking while fishing and fell asleep on the shore. Papa always wore his brown overalls when he fished, which turned out to be a fatal mistake because a herd of beavers mistook him for a log and gnawed off his limbs to use in their damn dam. Even used his head to plug a leaky section.

Mama was never the same after that.

Prom night came and I was wearing one of my father's suits – blue not brown obviously. I even got a corsage for Millie. We'd already gotten to first base and I was hoping to slide into second after the dance down at lover's lane. I told Mama that I was leaving to pick up my date. Mama looked so sad, then she collapsed to the floor twitching.

I got a damp cloth for her face and tried to wake her up. It worked, but then she rolled up her sleeves and skirt and started screaming when she saw red dots all over her skin. She kept yelling that she had the dread beaver pox.

I'd never heard of beaver pox before, but Mama laid there insisting that she had it and that the twice damned beavers were trying to kill her too. She told me she was in agony and that the pox made her unable to walk. Mama kept harping about how unfair it would be for the demon beavers to take both of my parents, especially if I left her there to die. She said the guilt might well kill me too and the beavers would have eliminated our whole bloodline, so I called up Millie and canceled our date. I have regretted it every day since, especially after I heard my buddy Ron say he got to third with her in the janitor's closet during the dance.

We called out Doc Parsons to take a look at mama. Turns out old Doc Parsons had never even heard of beaver pox, but you have to remember this was almost sixty years ago. People just didn't know about it back then. Even today the only real source of information on beaver pox is Mama's own website.

Luckily Mama had a bunch of what today they'd call homeopathic cures passed down to her from her granny and her granny's granny. Mostly they involved her laying with her head and feet elevated, eating bonbons, drinking lots of cool beverages and being fed food by someone else. And the never-ending foot rubs. For years I prayed for the pox to take her feet, so I'd never have to touch them again. I was never that lucky. The beaver pox has cursed us for years. Mind you, there were times that it didn't seem to bother mama much, but there always seemed to be a flare-up when I had plans to go out socially and I'd have to cancel. I've been canceling my plans for fifty-nine years and I'm sick of it. I want to go out and sow my wild oats. I want to be the one to get to third base with Milly Dunn, although her third husband and total hip replacement might make that a bit more challenging than it would have been back in high school.

I've broached the subject with mama every six months like

clockwork, but mama always has the same answer – I'd only have her for so long because the evil beaver pox would soon take her from this world and I'd be all alone. Well, I ain't buying it no more. Mama turned one hundred on her last birthday and the pox ain't taken her nowhere yet. In fact, one day when she thought I was taking a nap, she got up and walked around our house without a walker and she emptied out a bunch of big old frozen turkeys from the freezer to get to her pistachio and peanut butter ice cream. I think the beaver pox went away, but she's so used to being sick that maybe she don't know what it's like to be well.

And another thing – I always thought it was plenty odd that we had so many red pens and markers just lying about. I woke from another nap to see mama drawing with one on her own skin. I leapt to my feet and asked her what she was doing. She told me that the ink from the markers calms down the itching from the pox, but it sure looked to me like she was drawing them on. And if that done worked so well, how come I had to rub calamine lotion into her wrinkly old hide three times a day for almost sixty years? I'd know more, but mama won't let me go to her appointments and the doctors say they can't tell me nothing cause of those darn hippo and confidentiality laws. I still don't see what no hippo's got to do with medical records, though. It they tell, does the hippo sit on them or something?

What I need to know is can beaver pox go into remission? And do you think that they'll ever develop a vaccination for this dread disease? Mama says that sometimes it's often passed down through families and because my dad was killed by beavers and that she has the pox, that I have double the risk of getting it. As a matter of fact, one time about forty years ago I woke up with a bunch red dots all over my body. Let me tell you I was a bit freaked out, but mama was asleep and so I went in and took a shower. Luckily by the end of it, my red dots was gone.

Do you think I might get it? And do you think at a hundred mama can just get by on her own so I can go out and find me a wife and start my own family? Although I'm not sure if I want to have kids if they are going to get beaver pox. Mama says it can skip a generation, so maybe I'll get lucky. What do you think I should do?

– Beloved Son Battling Beaver Pox in Battle Creek

Dear Battle Creek,

Cthulhu must state that he is not a physician, but a quick search of the Internet found that you are correct – the only listing of beaver pox on the web is on your mother's website. This may be hard to hear, but by all appearances and from what you have written, it would seem that your mother concocted this fictional disease in order to manipulate and control you for nearly six decades. Perhaps it was the trauma of losing her husband or perhaps she is what you humans refer to as a conniving bitch. Whatever the reason, her actions have caused you to waste the majority of your pitifully short human existence.

However, all the blame does not lie with your mother. All humans, for good or usually ill, have free will. You could have left at any time and done what you wanted. You could have tried to have someone else watch her so you could have a social life. You could have actually spoken to other doctors and done your own research and found out that your mother was shoveling a load of beaver manure your way. You might have learned that there was no hippopotamus involvement in medical records and that the correct word was HIPAA, an acronym that I could not be bothered to tell you the meaning of. You could have learned a group of beavers is a colony, not a herd. You could have simply abandoned her. Instead, you allowed yourself to be manipulated by another, instead of standing up for your rights.

The red markers and pens are obviously what she uses to put the phony pox on her body. Regarding the time many years ago you woke up with red dots was most likely because your mother put them on you in an attempt to further control you and was short-sighted enough to not use permanent markers.

Not knowing your general health condition, I cannot say whether it is too late for you to start a family, but there have been human males older than you who have spawned children, so if you can find a human female young enough to still produce offspring and who is willing to procreate with someone with much more skin wrinklage than herself, then it is possible. You should consider that it is unlikely that you will alive for much of the child's life. You have already exceeded the average lifespan for a human male. However, if your genetic makeup allows you to live a comparable lifespan to your mother's, you may survive until the child at least graduates from high school.

Dear Cthulhu,

My family thinks I'm crazy, but I'm convinced I have leprosy. I know that the disease has been all but eliminated from the world and that they closed the only remaining leper colony in the United States.

For weeks now, seeping sores have appeared all over my body. Unfortunately, I come from a religious family who doesn't believe in going to doctors, so I haven't been able to get a medical opinion yet. But from what I've seen on the Internet it sure looks like leprosy. My family thinks I've just been doing my Bible studies too hard because the wounds happened to show up around the same time we read about Jesus healing the lepers. Our pastor thinks it's psychosomatic.

I think they're wrong and that I have leprosy. I haven't been out of the country, so where would I catch it? All I do go to school, work, go to church and raise prize armadillos.

What should I do?

– Leper in Fort Worth

Dear Fort Worth,

Cthulhu is a trifle unclear as to the meaning of your question as to what you should do. If you mean what should you do about your religion, perhaps you would consider joining the Cult of Cthulhu which is still holding on as the twelfth fastest growing religion in the world. Should you have leprosy, if would actually be a benefit for being one of my worshippers because Cthulhu does not eat diseased meat.

However, if you are referring to what you should do about your physical condition, you should likely seek medical attention. Cthulhu has not bothered since the last letter to get a medical degree and is not a doctor, although I once role-played as one on my last trip to The Tentacle Ranch outside of Las Vegas.

While faith in a higher power – preferably Cthulhu – is a wonderful thing, it is really no substitute for medical treatment, although it often disturbs Cthulhu to find that prayer to other entities besides myself not only brings comfort to people but sometimes actually helps them. Be that as it may, it does not matter that you have not left the country. There have been several recently diagnosed cases of leprosy in Texas. It seems that armadillos have been found to carry the disease beneath their shell plating, so not only should you get yourself checked but your prize pets as well. And should you decide that you would like to switch belief systems, do not hesitate to contact Cthulhu.

Dear Cthulhu,

My wife and I recently have been getting into trouble with our neighbors and local authorities because of our decisions on how we raise our children. We've decided to go back to a better and simpler time and raise our offspring as free range children, just like in the good old days.

Apparently, some of our busy-body neighbors object to this and have been having the police hound us because our children walk to school on their own through our safe suburban neighborhood. They tell us it's unsafe, yet there hasn't been a violent crime reported here in years and there has never been a child abduction reported in our town ever.

Do you think we're doing the right thing raising our children free range?

– Free Rangers In Fredonia

Dear Free Rangers,

Cthulhu is with you one hundred percent. I actually admire what you are doing. In today's environment, children are herded in and out of schools and fed all sorts of artificial additives which really taint their taste. The idea that you are raising free range children is amazing to Cthulhu. Thank you. Children are so much tastier when they are free range – I simply cannot tell you how wonderful this is. And the lack of violent crime helps assure they survive long enough to make it to market. I'm not sure what age you are planning to sell them off for food, but Cthulhu would like to put an order in now.

Dear Cthulhu,

I read with interest a recent letter because I have a similar problem. My marriage has gone to the dogs – literally. My husband and I were watching a local talk show on TV. They had on one of those comedian hypnotists demonstrating his act and he hypnotized one of the hosts into thinking he was a dog. Had him bark, roll over and beg – that sort of thing. I thought it was stupid and turned the TV off to go make dinner when I heard the pitter patter of something behind me and realized my husband was following me on hands and knees. I rolled my eyes and told "Jack" he was very funny, then he barked at me, but he kept up with the act. He wouldn't eat at the table so I had to put his dinner and a bowl of beer on the floor. I figured enough was enough and went back in and turned the TV back on.

Sadly, the segment was over and they had moved on to a woman in a bikini who juggled guinea pigs, water balloons, and machetes to raise money for a charity to save the manatees.

I went back in to check on Jack, worried he was going to choke, but he finished his whole steak and was even gnawing on the bone.

When I went to sleep, Jack came to bed at the same time and crawled up on my feet. It was the first time that had happened in years. Usually, he stays up on his computer. Jack claims he's playing video poker, but I really doubted virtual card players scream and moan that loudly.

Things got a little awkward in the morning. Jack licked my face to wake me up, which is the most romantic he's been since our honeymoon. Next, he ran and whined by the back door. Judging by the way he crossed his legs he had to go potty, but he wouldn't use the bathroom. I told him enough was enough and he needed to snap out of it. I even snapped my fingers a couple times like I'd seen done on sitcoms, but he stayed a dog.

Jack started whining and howling. Our apartment is half of a house and I didn't want to wake our neighbor who was also our landlord, so I opened the back door. Jack ran outside and began marking his territory. He had just been wearing a pair of pajama pants with an easy open fly in the front, plus he had been going commando so he was able to manage it without having to unzip or undress.

My husband has been unemployed since he got laid off from his job at the Whoopie Pie factory. These days I am the main breadwinner and I don't get sick days. That meant I had to go to work or we'd be out on the street.

Even though Jack was acting like a dog, I figured deep inside he was still a grown man, so he'd be safe to leave at home alone, right?

Wrong! I came back from work and Jack had chewed up all the newspapers from the recycling bin and pooped behind the couch. I yelled at him and figured that would be the end of it, right?

Wrong again. When I came home from work the next night he chewed up my only pair of good dress shoes and pooped again, this time in the dining room. If Jack was going to act like a dog, I was going to treat him like one. I was not about to keep cleaning up man poop, so I rubbed his nose in it. Then I took him over and rubbed his nose in my chewed shoes, then hit him several times on the nose with a newspaper. He whimpered and rolled over on his back and was so pathetic I found myself actually feeling bad for him.

On day three, the shower curtain was torn down and he had pooped in the tub.

All right, at least it was easier to clean, but I wasn't going to be able to put up with much more man poop cleanup.

I don't make enough to hire a dog sitter, so I called our neighbor/landlord "Rose". When I told her what was happening, she rushed over to see it for herself. Hubby barked at Rose, sniffed her crotch, then jumped up so his "front paws" landed on her boobs. The jerk was copping a feel in front of me and Rose didn't even care. She was too busy rubbing his head, scratching behind his ears and making his left leg twitch. Jack licked her on the cheek, then on the lips. I yelled at him to get down, but Rose only laughed and said it was okay. Then she told him he was a good dog and rubbed his belly. He rolled over and started panting. I invited her to sit down for coffee and asked her if she'd be willing to watch him while I worked. Rose agreed.

I got up to use the bathroom. When I came back, Jack was humping her leg. Rose said it was okay and joked that was the most action she had gotten in a while. I'll admit I was more than a little jealous – that was more action than I'd gotten in a very long while too. I found myself looking at my legs and wondering why my dog of a husband didn't think they were humpable and realized I wasn't the only one in this marriage with issues.

Things went well for a week. I'd come home to find them playing fetch in the yard or her walking him around it – Rose had gone out and bought Jack a collar and leash. Jack seemed to love them. Rose also bought him real dog food and he was actually eating it. At night when Rose left, he'd spend ten minutes whimpering at the door and then curled up into a ball on the mat.

By the time that Saturday came, I'd had enough. I went online and found a recorded version of the show which I hoped would include the hypnotist bringing the host out of the hypnotic state and returning him to normal. The problem was, I couldn't get Jack to sit in front of the computer screen to watch it. He kept bring me a chew toy Rose had bought him, wanting me to throw it.

Even though I hated doing it, I called Rose and asked her to come over to help. Rose sat in a chair facing the computer screen and put my husband's back between her legs and his front "paws" up on the table and made him watch it. At the end, the host was back to normal, but my husband still thought he was a dog.

Wait, it gets worse. Apparently Rose watched it too closely and now she thought she was a dog. She dropped down to all fours was crawling around the room barking. My husband went up to her and started sniffing her butt, then she did the same.

Before I could figure things out, I got an emergency call to go into work. I didn't know what to do. The backyard was fenced in and it was a warm sunny day, so I left them in the yard. I wasn't cleaning up man and woman poop.

When I got back, they were both naked and he was doing a lot more than humping her leg. I yelled at him to get off of her, but neither would listen. If they were going to act like animals, that's how I was going to treat them. I got out the hose and sprayed them until they broke apart. I chased Rose back to her apartment and Jack back to ours. Next, I turned and screamed in frustration as I saw that both of them in pooped in the backyard. I'd had enough and just left it there.

I'm at my wits end. I'd leave him, but the apartment is in my name and where am I going to go? I don't have family or any friends who would let me move in with them. Do you think I could drop the two of them off at an animal shelter? Would they take them? I'm tempted to just lock the both of them in Rose's apartment with a bag of kibble, but I'm afraid I'd get in trouble for people abuse.

How can I turn Jack back? Rose I'm mad at and don't really care about what happens to her.

– Married to a Dog in Des Moines

Dear Des Moines,

Cthulhu believes animal shelters have rules about taking in human beings. Otherwise, people who were homeless would start going to them. Which would not be a bad thing. Judging by what Cthulhu has seen of humanity, they would be treated better in an animal shelter than they would at a people shelter, at least at the ones that don't euthanise the animals.

Assuming your husband is legitimately hypnotized, you have several options. In general, hypnosis is not permanent. Hypnotic suggestions wear off in time, but it does not sound like you are looking to wait.

A better idea would be to either contact a local professional hypnotherapist or the talk show to see if they can put you in touch with the performer. Either way, have somebody put him under and then take them out of his hypnotic state. This should return him to normal. Another thing you should consider is that your husband is not actually hypnotized and that everything he is doing is an act. Humans crack. You would not believe the number of people who have mental breakdowns after meeting me for the first time. Honestly, if Cthulhu actually cared about what humans thought, it might give me a complex.

In your husband's case, perhaps the pressures of life got to him after losing his job. Maybe some part of him felt life as a canine companion would be preferable to that as a person. It is also quite possible that he had had a procreation longing towards your landlord prior to this and simply used things to his advantage. She, on the other hand, is likely not hypnotized but found it intriguing to have a simple animalistic relationship with no strings attached, nor the need for any conversation or pressure to commit. From many of the letters Cthulhu gets, there are plenty of humans who would be perfectly happy if they could simply get procreation with none of the other additional social niceties that tend to be involved with the pre-and post- procreation mating rituals.

Cthulhu would like to point out that part of the situation you are in is your own doing. It is obvious from your letter that you did not put much effort into your marriage or spend much quality time together. Whether the acting like a dog was from a mental instability or hypnosis, it may have been your husband's way of crying out for help. He may have felt isolated and lonely. When he came to bed with you that first night, did you play with him or pet him? Or try anything to make him feel better? Or was it all about how his actions were affecting you? Your husband, like most humans, wanted attention and to feel special and needed. Utter nonsense as none of you are special and are only really needed as a source of amusement to Cthulhu. Regardless, you didn't bother to play with him.

On the other tentacle, your landlord petted and rubbed him, possibly his first affectionate human touch in years. Is it any wonder he tried to procreate with her leg? It was not the shape or look of the limb, but the human contact. Then she took the time to take him for walks and play fetch. Had you done these things, his non-martial limb humping might never have happened. Perhaps if the hypnotist brings him back to normal, you should consider spending more quality time with each other. You are likely just in need of it as he is.

If the hypnotist is unable to end his canine behavior, the best remaining method to snap him out of it would be to take him to a vet. Once in the waiting room, mention that you are there to get him neutered. If he is faking, that should bring him out of it. If he is not, at least he will not have any more procreational interest in your landlord.

Dear Cthulhu,

I wrote to you recently regarding the troubles my wife and I were having in regards to getting pregnant and our difficulty adopting kids due to our lack of funds. When last I wrote, I was in jail on prostitution and trumped up baby trafficking charges for asking prostitutes to consider letting us adapt their children should they ever become pregnant.

I admit I didn't take your advice to plead guilty to the solicitation charge to get a slap on the wrist and go home. I come from a religious family where such a thing would be very shameful, even if it wasn't true.

Luckily, all the charges were dropped thanks to a good judge. Turns out the cops who did the sting had recorded the whole thing. They hadn't introduced the video as evidence, relying on the undercover officer's testimony. My public defender was too stupid to ask to see the recording.

As luck would have it, I was arraigned right after another gentleman was caught in the same sting. They used a video showing that he had requested not only the services of three prostitutes but a goat, a vacuum cleaner, a beehive and an inflatable vibrating teddy bear.

The judge asked if my arrest was from the same sting operation and then asked my lawyer if he had seen the video. He admitted he hadn't, so the recording was played. It clearly showed that I was telling the truth and although I did give the prostitutes money, it was only so I could speak to them about possible adoptions. Luckily, paying people to talk to you isn't illegal and all the charges were dropped. Unfortunately, one of the reporters in the courtroom found it fascinating and wrote a feature in the paper that my wife read. I hadn't told her about the arrest or about who I was speaking to regarding adoption. She wasn't sure if she believed me when I told her I hadn't been with any of those women. After I finally convinced her by showing her a transcript of the court hearings, I dove in head first and mentioned your advice about me having an affair in order to impregnate another woman. My wife slapped me across the face, then moved back home with her mother.

My wife is the love of my life and her leaving hit me hard. And her slap did too. I started drinking heavily. One night while I was extremely drunk, I started trolling the Internet for a way to adopt a baby that wouldn't cost as much as a small house, which was far more money than we had.

Then an online miracle happened. I found an adoption site that was totally and absolutely free. Admittedly, there was a lot of alcohol in my system and the screen was not only blurry, but there appeared to be two of them, but I wasn't one to look a gift horse in the mouth. I filled out the form and was instantly approved for the adoption. They even emailed me a certificate.

Even though it was two the morning, I drunk dialed my wife and told her the news. She was so excited and happy, that she came right home and we made mad passionate love.

The next morning, I overslept for work and had to leave without taking a shower or eating breakfast, but I made it to work on time. I didn't have a chance to check my email for the adoption papers until lunchtime. It was then I realized my mistake.

I hadn't signed up to adopt a child. I hadn't signed up to adopt a dog or cat either. Instead, I managed to adopt a one-mile section of highway near our house.

I called my wife to try and explain my mistake, but before I could say anything she started telling me about how she's told her entire family, friends, and everybody in town that were going to be parents.

If I tell her the truth, I know I'm going to lose her and be a laughingstock. But if I don't tell her, she'll figure it out when no baby arrives. Should I kidnap a child? I could drive several hours away.

I know you mentioned that you managed to get a woman to let you adopt her baby. Do you think you can help a guy out and hook me up? Please? Or even let me adopt that baby from you. I'd be eternally grateful.

– Even More Paternally Perturbed Man in Modesto

Dear Perturbed,

Letting you adopt him is no longer an option. Sadly, my adopted son – who incidentally I named Delicious – is no longer with us, although he lingered with me for days. It was a painful loss, mainly because Delicious gave me such heartburn. And Cthulhu has not gotten any letters recently from people trying to get rid of their unwanted or tasty children. Although that in and of itself is an oddity. As I mentioned to you in my response to your previous letter, human parenting is a thankless and heartbreaking task. Every few months I get a letter from a parent wanting to get rid of their children in some way, shape, or form. Amazingly, few are actually willing to go through with it in the end, some out of misguided love and others from a fear that the authorities might prosecute them.

I do not recommend kidnapping a child. Fifty years ago it may have worked, but today in the information age, any missing child will have an Amber alert issued and anyone with a new baby will eventually meet someone who starts asking questions and is intelligent and nosy enough to call a tip line. After a quick round of genetic testing, there will be no doubt as to your crime.

I do not believe you will be able to procure a baby in time to placate your wife and adopting a pet will not be the same, especially for a human female who feels motherhood is passing her by.

Cthulhu reiterates that your best bet for a child is to impregnate another woman, then sue for joint custody.

Barring that, go out and purchase one of those "It's a Boy" signs with a stork on it and put it out on your stretch of highway and bring your wife by and explain what happened. Perhaps she will have a sense of humor about it. Or, more likely, file for divorce. Of course, that will leave you unencumbered to go out and try to impregnate other women. And if you are successful in gaining custody, you can use the child as a lure to re-kindle your romance with your wife. Or perhaps you will find you enjoy the new and fertile female more than your barren and unsupportive one.

Dear Cthulhu,

I'm a straight C student. Unfortunately, I'm the child of two overachievers. Both my parents were valedictorians of their high school class. My mom's a rocket scientist. My dad is a brain surgeon. They are constantly on my case about my grades, trying to motivate and force me to work harder, telling me that I'm never going to get into a decent college. This despite the fact that I really do study hard. The problem is I was diagnosed with dyslexia and I have trouble reading. However, I excel in areas they never did. I'm the pitcher for my school's baseball team and can throw a 92 MPH fastball. I'm also class president and a member of the chess club. My parents taught me the game soon after I was able to walk. It's the one area where I'm actually better than the two of them. Whenever we play, I set up two boards and play them both at the same time. I haven't lost since I was eight.

For years, I pointed out that I'm good enough to get a scholarship to college for baseball, which likely means they would overlook C grades. I would also qualify for a scholarship for chess. They're few and far between, but they do exist. It wasn't enough for them.

Because of cuts in federal funding, when teachers retired at my school, they didn't replace them. Instead, existing teachers had to double up, so my math and science teacher was the same woman, Ms. "Galore". Ms. Galore is also the faculty advisor to the chess club. A few months back on my 18th birthday, I was the only one on the chess team who made nationals. I spent a lot of time practicing with Ms. Galore and we became very close. I even gave her a shoulder to cry on when her husband divorced her for a college cheerleader.

The chess club raised enough money for me and one other person to travel to Las Vegas for nationals. I asked my parents to go. Mom was working on a reusable rocket design for a private corporation and Dad had been asked to give a talk at the local elementary school on career day, so they both said no. Despite all their other accomplishments, I honestly think there are some jealousy issues on their part. They met playing chess and like I said neither of them –even both of them working together – have been able to beat me since I was a kid.

So I asked Ms. Galore and she said yes.

Despite all the raised money, there was only enough to pay for one hotel room, so we had to share.

The night before the tournament I was real nervous and couldn't stop pacing. Ms. Galore suggested we play a game of chess to calm me down. I beat her in 12 moves and didn't stop pacing the whole time.

Ms. Galore had been trying to teach me to play with distractions, so she suggested we play strip chess. It was like a dream come true. Ms. Galore was the hottest woman I've ever seen in real life. It worked because I lost my shirt in the first game, but after that, I beat the pants off her. Then the blouse and bra. I was distracted again and lost everything but my boxers before I starting winning again and finally beat her thong off her, leaving her naked.

She stood to give me a congratulatory hug. When I stood my boxers had a very distinct shape. Ms. Galore looked down and smiled and the hug ended up leading to something else much more intimate and wonderful.

The next day at the national chess tournament not only did I win, but I did it in record time. I was motivated. Ms. Galore promised to let me try anything I wanted with her back at the hotel if I won the tournament and I was in a hurry to take her up on the offer. So basically after the check, we got to mate. Again.

I got a trophy and a small award ceremony when I got back to the school. The tournament was in November and ever since then my grades in math and physics jumped to perfect scores.

My parents were thrilled, although they still give me grief over my other C classes. I've gotten several scholarship offers for baseball and two for chess. One of the schools offering a chess scholarship would even let me bring my coach up to the college level with me. And I'm seriously considering bringing Ms. Galore, because not everything that happens in Vegas stays in Vegas, although she is refusing to go to prom with me. She's afraid of losing her job and teaching license.

The problem is I know I didn't earn those A's, at least not in the traditional sense. I'm torn about whether or not I should confess, but I don't want anything to happen to Ms. Galore or to lose my scholarship offers. And I would love to bring her to college with me to keep me motivated, but the baseball scholarship is to a better school and covers everything, while the chess one only covers tuition.

What should I do?

-Chess Player in Cleveland

Dear Chess,

You may be thinking with the wrong body part. Confession will do nothing positive for anyone involved. You did earn your grades even if it was not in the traditionally accepted way. For centuries men had been trading money, prestige and other favors to women in return for procreational acts. In recent years, women have been getting in on the act. You seemed pleased with the results, are of legal age, and were not forced, so keep your mouth shut.

Cthulhu recommends not bringing Ms. Galore to college with you. You may meet someone your own age with whom you want to procreate. Or you may both decide that you are both in the nonsense called love and want to be together, which would still get her fired as few colleges will let their staff procreate with students. Since you are no longer her student, you might be able to formally date her.

Also, it might be disturbing to you if she meets other men at the college closer to her age and decides to teach them how to work through distractions the same way she did you.

Dear Cthulhu,

I am a Second Amendment advocate (I hate the term gun nut). I've been collecting firearms ever since my father gave me my first rifle on my 3rd birthday. I own over 300 rifles, shotguns and automatic weapons plus another 150 handguns, both revolvers and automatics. I have more stored ammunition than the New Mexico National Guard.

It's more than just a hobby with me – it's a fashion statement. My handgun collection comes in a number of styles and colors. I may carry concealed, but that's no reason for my gun to clash with my outfit. I, of course, have all the necessary permits to carry concealed.

Then I realized that I had all this wonderful armament and because I live alone, no one ever gets to see it. A few times I invited some friends over and showed off my collection, but they all got very nervous and made excuses to leave. Which is a shame, because I had bought a lovely bunch of guns to give out as parting gifts. Their loss.

Then I met a few guys who had been stationed in Afghanistan and had snuck some neat things out of the country. They sold me my very own rocket launcher. Cthulhu, you should see this baby. It is beyond awesome. It could take out a helicopter, plane or tractor-trailer. I had a neighbor who needed some land cleared and was gonna pay a lot of money to knock down some trees. I did it for free.

I love this thing more than I've loved any other object or person in my life. I sleep with it, sit it in a chair at the table when I eat with a napkin tied around its neck. I even put up a special wall hook in the bathroom so I didn't have to be apart from "Launchy" when I showered. The only time I was away from Launchy was when I worked. The more I thought about it, the more I realize that it was stupid to leave Launchy home just because I had a job. I mean lots of other people bring stuff to work like purses and cell phones. Why shouldn't I be able to bring a rocket launcher?

So I did. Unfortunately, the principal of the school where I work as a second-grade teacher objected and called the cops on me. I was arrested and they got a search warrant for my house. When they found my collection, they seized it and locked me up without bail. And without Launchy.

It's just not fair, I tell you. Now they think I'm a danger to the kids. Did anyone ask the kids what they thought? From what the rugrats told me, it was the greatest show and tell ever.

I have looked to the American Rifle Association for assistance, but even they are not willing to help me because I brought it to a school and it's not technically a gun.

So Cthulhu tell me – do you feel taking rocket launchers to an elementary school is covered by the Second Amendment or not?

– Gun and Rocket Launcher Advocate in Albuquerque.

Dear Gun Nut,

As a whole, Cthulhu is amused by the laws of humankind. My understanding is the original intent of the Second Amendment was to prevent tyranny, using the logic that it would be harder to conquer people who could shoot back. Nothing in there gives you the right to bring a weapon to show and tell with children.

As far as the stockpiling of weapons goes, Cthulhu has no objections to small arms as I am impervious to them. Cthulhu is not found of nuclear weapons. Not only can they give me a bad sunburn, but they poison the planet I will one day rule or destroy, not to mention kill off the people who are fated to serve me and serve as my source of nourishment and amusement. So I do not care about your having the weapons you mentioned, so long as you do not use any on other humans, who are by rights mine.

It appears that you have lost touch with the reality that most of your fellow humans share. There have been a number of senseless gun-related tragedies, several involving children in schools. Bringing any kind of weapon to school violates not only your school district's likely zero tolerance weapons policy but common sense as well. Children are humanity's future and my future subjects and snacks and as such should be protected and well-seasoned.

It does appear to Cthulhu as though you had no plans to actually use the weapon. However, most other people would not realize that. You were fortunate to have been taken alive all things considered.

Instead of bringing the weapon to work, you should have opened up a gun museum and put the pieces on display. That way fellow gun nuts could come admire your hardware without any perceived threat of injury to others. A pity you didn't write to Cthulhu before show and tell. It seems likely that you will be convicted and convicted felons are typically banned from owning firearms and it would most certainly be a condition of any parole. You will have to take up a new hobby. Have you considered taxidermy, cockroach racing or stamp collecting? Maybe trying to get a complete collection of every Dear Cthulhu column and book ever published will help fill the void.

Dear Cthulhu,

My girlfriend has always been more than a bit on the weird side. When we started dating that's one of the things that first attracted me to her. We'd go to parties where all the other women would be wearing a little black dress and "Lorna" would have a Starfleet uniform or medieval princess outfit on. She has a tendency to get a little too involved in whatever aspect of fandom she is fancying at the time. Which is not necessarily a bad thing, especially when I got her started watching some sci-fi porn. She'd do almost anything we saw onscreen, which is how our problem started.

Her latest love is steampunk. Believe it or not, there's quite a bit of steampunk porn on the Internet. True, it gets a little cliché at times, with all the guys wearing goggles and top hats and the women carrying parasols that turn into guns, although the corsets are pretty cool.

The problem started after we watched *I, Steambot*. It was set in a mythical Victorian England, where our heroine must build a robot to stop a horde of overly endowed and oversexed male zombies from taking the virginity away from London's young women. Let's just say the zombies' hunger wasn't for brains. In the end, the heroine wins and her robot destroys the zombies.

It must have been pretty successful because they made a sequel – *O, Steambot*. There's a new plot – apparently, the zombie plague only affected men and the steambot wiped them all out. Now London's young and no longer virginal women are upset, horny, and missing their lovers' endless supply of rigor mortis members and they blame the heroine.

Since a subplot of the first movie had the heroine as one of the first victims which motivated her to build the bot, we find out she is feeling the same way, so she adapts her robot to service the disappointed women's needs. By attaching what looks like a miniature vibrating jackhammer to the steambot's lower body, then making other modifications for his head and limbs, the new and improved steambot can service multiple women at the same time.

For porn, the special effects were very realistic.

After watching *I, Steambot*, Lorna had me dress up as a zombie in the bedroom for a month. After *O, Steambot* she had me dress up as a robot, but that wasn't enough for her. Lorna built a steam-powered love toy that fit over my own man equipment. For the first few minutes the vibrating was good for both of us, but then the inside overheated I got some second-degree burns in a very delicate area. The ER doctor told me I couldn't have sex for 2 to 3 months until everything healed.

That was too long for Lorna to do without. After the first week, she began getting a little stir crazy. She started tinkering in the basement where she keeps her engineering lab – she has an engineering doctorate and designs satellite robot arms and such for a living.

Then, Lorna took a week off from work and locked herself down there. She didn't come up for days and with a fridge, microwave, and a bathroom she didn't really have to.

I went on with my life as best I could. With my nether region boiled and blistered, I was on some pretty powerful pain meds. I slept a lot. One night I woke to the sound of Lorna screaming like she was being killed. I quickly rushed downstairs, but the basement was locked, so I broke the door down and ran into the basement.

I had assumed Lorna was in trouble. She wasn't. What I thought were screams of pain were actually those of pleasure. Lorna had built her own steambot sex toy and had even improved upon the movie's design. The robot was bolted into a platform which had a table which could serve as a chair, bed, or whatever else was needed depending on where it was positioned. The robot could pivot itself for different positions. The bot was vibrating so fast I could have thrown ice on it and made margaritas.

I yelled at Lorna and asked her what the hell she was doing, but either she didn't notice me or she ignored me for another half-hour as she carried on with her robot lover.

I looked for a plug to pull to stop it, but the power source was contained in the platform, so I was forced to watch as this device pleasured my woman. Part of me wanted to destroy it, but another part was aroused, which hurt so I had to go upstairs and pop another pain pill and get some burn cream.

When Lorna was finally done, I confronted her, but she was sweaty, exhausted and couldn't stop smiling.

I asked her how she could cheat on me. You know what she said? It wasn't cheating because the steambot wasn't a person. She said it was the same thing as her using a sex toy. We argued for an hour, but she refused to see reason.

She pointed out that I couldn't do anything with her for at least another month. I pointed out that my burns were her fault and that I'd offered her other options which she turned down.

Lorna refused to give up her steambot. Even worse, she invited her best friend over – the one who always dresses in white blouses, plaid skirts, and ponytails – and the two of them went down to the basement for the entire night. I'd been trying to get her to invite that friend for a threesome for years and she never did. Yet she does it for a hunk of metal and steam instead. And to top it off, they wouldn't even let me watch. Which, considering the pain it would have caused my neither regions, was probably for the best.

To make a long story short, fast forward to now. I healed up two months ago and I still haven't gotten any action at all. Lorna is even talking about patenting her steambot and selling it to women. She's improved on her first design, giving the thing four arms that can lift, move, grope and spank. Plus, she's added a purée function. She says she'll still keep me around to take out the garbage, mow the lawn and kill mice. I've about had it. Part of me feels that I have a duty to all the guys out there to destroy this steambot before he gets on the market.

Do you think I should destroy the steambot? Should I break up with Lorna or do you think if I break her bot that she'll come back to me? And lastly, am I right that she's technically cheating on me?

– Being Steampunked in My Own House

Dear Steampunked,

Destroying the steambot would only make your girlfriend have to go and build another one and this one might have even newer attachments and improvements. I would personally recommend tentacles as it has been Cthulhu's experience that human women can't get enough of them. At least I assume that's what all that screaming means.

As for whether you should break up with her, it depends on whether or not you are able to accept being in a platonic relationship and knowing that your girlfriend found your procreation skills so lacking that she had to go out and build herself a man-sized sex toy.

As to whether or not it is cheating, I agree with your girlfriend. It would only be cheating if it was with another person or perhaps another living thing. So long as she doesn't figure out how to give the robot artificial intelligence, she is not procreating with another being. Although she may have cheated on you with her girlfriend that night in the basement, but you do not seem upset over that. In Cthulhu's experience, many men are willing to overlook their female significant others procreating with other females, particularly if they are allowed to be involved or at least video the activities.

Cthulhu does have a solution for you that would not involve you having to destroy the steambot or break up with your girlfriend. Simply ask her if she would design a female steambot to satisfy your needs – being careful to insulate the inside so as not to cause further injury to your procreative part. Then the two of you can play with your toys and she will still have someone to mow the lawn and take out the garbage and you can pretend that you have a woman that cares about you.

Dear Cthulhu,

It's me, NecroPhil again. I just wrote to you about mistakenly banging my dead wife's identically dead twin sister. We had the funeral, they were buried and I went home. As I mentioned, Gemini and I were both sex addicts, bumping nasties multiple times a day.

Well, it'd been four days since she died and I'd only had sex once and it wasn't even with her. I became obsessed with not having given her that one last send-off to the afterlife. Plus, I couldn't get out of my mind how good it was being the one to call the shots, so I snuck into the cemetery last night. I work with heavy machinery, so had no problems digging up her grave. The dirt was still fresh; they hadn't even put the tombstones up. I climbed into the hole, opened the coffin and looked down at her as the moonlight glistened on her cold skin. Even dead, she was still the prettiest woman I've ever seen.

Once again I undressed the lower body and proceeded to rock her afterworld. It was better than the first time as I was able to position her and all sorts of ways and do things she would never let me do in real life. As was our custom, I laid down to cuddle with her in the afterglow, but when I went to pinch her left nipple ring, it wasn't there.

I'd slept with her sister. Again.

It was dark and there were no grave markers, but shouldn't I still have known? Once was an accident, but twice is a pattern. Do you think I'm really in love with my wife's identical twin sister? And do you think would be okay if I went back tonight and dug up my actual wife? I could apologize and have sex with her corpse three times to make it up to her – once for each of the times I banged her twin and once for the sendoff. I figure I'll just fake the first two times – I'm not a teenager anymore, plus she's dead so she probably won't notice. What do you think? Is what I've done wrong? Or is there something wrong with me?

– NecroPhil

Dear NecroPhil,

You ask if Cthulhu thinks you have done something wrong. Unless you cut in front of the twin sister's husband who was waiting to have sex with her corpse, it is a victimless crime.

As for if there is something wrong with you – you are trying to procreate with a corpse after procreating with another identical dead human. For humans, this behavior is considered wrong. For others races, not so much. Mi-go have no issues with it. Live dolphins know not to turn their backs on a deep one, while the dead ones aren't so lucky. Then again, I've heard of live dolphins doing the same back to the deep ones and tourists who pay to swim with the porpoises. I assume you are human, so culturally speaking the answer is yes.

As to whether or not you slept with your sister-in-law again on purpose, Cthulhu suggests that perhaps you have some unresolved issues with your departed wife and her being deceased leaves you with no way to resolve them so you are getting back at her by having intimate relations with her deceased twin.

Both your wife and sister-in-law are beyond caring about what happens to their corporal forms. However, instead of going to the time and effort to dig up corpses to procreate with, have you considered the bar scene? Or perhaps a dating site? Or a brothel? Maybe a street corner in a bad part of town. My understanding is that for humans procreation tends to be more enjoyable when both parties are actively participating and somewhat care for the other person, even if only for those few moments.

If it is indeed something you are trying to get back at your wife for, perhaps you could hook up with one of her living relatives and get the same satisfaction without desecrating a corpse.

Dear Cthulhu,

My sister has always had a vivid imagination. There were times in our childhood where she spent entire months living as if she were some make-believe character. Oddly, she only picked men characters to imitate, but then changed the names around so that they became women. At various times she was King Arthina, Robyn Hood, Jenny James, and Paula Bunyan. I tried to get Dad to stop her with that last one, saying she'd hurt herself with the ax, but he refused, saying he needed a section of our woods cleared. And we did make enough money selling firewood that year to buy an RV.

Everyone from my parents to our teachers thought it was adorable. She graduated first in her class in high school, finished college in five years with a doctorate and invented an app for cell phones that made her extremely rich.

What's the problem? She's back at it again. This time, she believes she's Sherley Holmes, the master Victorian detective. She set up a shingle and offered to solve mysteries for people. She even sucked me in to play the role of her Watson. I'd stop, except she lets me live in her house on our town's Baker Street for free and I get all my meals too, which means if she kicked me out I'd have to move and get a job.

I'm only concerned for my sister. Her little mystery solving endeavor has made it into the local papers and newscasts. I'm afraid people are laughing at her. Sure, she did manage to catch that one serial killer and uncover the loot from a bank robbery from back in the 1920s, but both of those were probably luck. I can't even talk to our parents because sis sent them on an around the world cruise with some of the reward money from both of those cases and they won't be back for a couple of years.

Can I have my sister committed? For her own safety, of course. And if I do, as her closest relative, that means I get control over her money and can do whatever I want with it, right?

– Concerned Sister in Chicago.

Dear Concerned,

In order to have someone committed, you typically need to prove that they are a danger to themselves or others. Your sister sounds like she is neither. As for becoming her power of attorney, you would either have to be appointed by her while she was still in her right mind or by the courts. Even then, you are still responsible for giving an accounting for all funds and how they were spent. However, it is a bureaucracy and it might be some time before any misdoings were found out.

Instead of scheming against your sibling, embrace it. View it as a game. Work to keep your sister happy, because if her mind reverts back to who she is and she learns that you been plotting against her, you may lose your cushy life and the only mystery you will have to solve then is who would want to hire you and whether you should live under an overpass or in a cardboard box.

Dear Cthulhu,

I'm seven years old. This summer, my family and I are going to spend a couple weeks up in the Finger Lakes area. My brother tells me that they're called that because they filled with real fingers. I think he's lying to try and freak me out.

What's the real story?

– Curious in Cortland

Dear Cortland,

The Finger Lakes got their name many years ago because of a bizarre human courtship ritual. Beautiful women would go to stand near the lake shore in skimpy bathing suits. Gentlemen callers would approach them and attempt to impress the women, often with gifts of gold, jewelry, and sometimes tracts of land.

There came a time when a competition arose among two determined suitors about who was more in love with a certain young woman. Each of them pledged their fortunes and their very lives, but the woman was unimpressed. After many displays of wealth and privilege, one man was driven to such desperation to prove his love and devotion that he stood over a lake, took out a knife and cut off his own finger. He let it fall into the water. His incredibly idiotic act of self-mutilation won the lady's heart and they were soon wed. As is apt to happen among humans, this stupidity inspired more and even greater idiocy. For years thereafter men – and the occasional woman – would attempt to prove their love and devotion to their significant others by coming to the lakes, cutting off a finger and letting it sink down into the black depths of the murky waters. This is one of the reasons they say the fish there still have a taste for human flesh. This was despite the fact that the original couple's marriage did not last. She cheated on her husband with their milkman. The husband in his rage decapitated his wife and put her head in the man's milk vats. Strangely they did not change the brand name to Decapitation Milk, start making human headcheese or the like.

Sadly, in recent years the finger slicing tradition has fallen out of favor and is frowned upon. But now you know the reason they named them the Finger Lakes.

That or because the lakes look like fingers when viewed on a map. I often get the two explanations mixed up.

Dear Cthulhu,

This is my third time writing you. I'm the gentleman who was mistakenly arrested for soliciting a prostitute while trying to convince workers to let me adopt their babies and then accidentally adopted a stretch of highway instead of a child while web surfing drunk.

I tried what you suggested and put an "It's a Girl" sign on the stretch of highway I adopted. My wife had always wanted a daughter. My wife did not find it amusing and in fact beat me unconscious with the stork sign. When I woke up in the hospital three days later, there were divorce papers waiting for me, taped on the IV stand.

My former wife is the love of my life and I feel I've failed her. I came up with another idea or two. First, I looked into becoming a foster parent but then found out that even abusive parents do not lose their parental rights and foster children can be taken out of a good home and returned to the family that hurt them in the first place because a judge felt that the abusers had reformed their ways. It may be selfish of me, but I can't allow myself to love a child that could then be ripped away from me. And my wife would snap and I'd prefer not to be beaten into another coma.

Instead, I started trolling hospitals for terminally ill, single mothers. I found one with a six-month-old baby. The father had lied about his name for a one night stand and run off. The woman had been diagnosed with cancer while she was pregnant and opted not to get treatment until after her daughter was born. Thankfully for me, it doesn't look like the chemo or radiation is helping her. I took a job as a hospice aide and managed to get myself assigned to her as a live-in. Not only am I taking care of "Linda" but I'm also helping out with her little bundle of joy, "Boo".

My plan was simple — to make her think of me as her best friend, then fall head over heels in love with me so that she would name me Boo's guardian when she died.

I fed them and changed both their diapers. I bonded with Boo and did everything possible for Linda. I've told her she was beautiful when she was frail and bald. I held her at night when she cried at the unfairness of it all. I even made love to her when she was vulnerable on numerous occasions. And for the first time in my life, I had sex without a condom. You recommended I go out and get another woman pregnant. Well, I figured if I got Linda pregnant and I was lucky enough for her to live long enough to deliver the baby, I'd definitely get custody when she died. So far, the cancer drugs seem to be stronger than my sperm, that hasn't stopped me from trying.

Despite my gallant efforts, things are not working out for me to be named Boo's guardian. It turns out that Linda has a sister who she's very close to and already named her guardian. I broached the subject of changing the guardian to me in an *I'd be happy to help you out kind of way*. I even pointed out that since Boo had bonded with me it might be better for the child to not lose both the stable adults in her young life. While she agreed that was true, she pointed out that she hadn't known me that long and she knew her sister would take good care of her daughter.

I secretly recorded Linda watching me take care of the child and saying what a good what a good parent that I'd be. I also made audio recordings of several conversations and have managed to splice together something that sounds like a deathbed declaration where she names me Boo's guardian. In fact, I've had to help her write checks to pay her bills and managed to get her to sign guardianship papers when she thought she was signing a payment for the electric bill. It turns out that my public defender from my prostitution trial had gotten fired. He wasn't very good at his job, but he did actually pass the bar. I offered him a few hundred bucks to draw up the guardianship papers and another five hundred to lie and testify after Linda dies that he saw her sign them. I figure that's enough to at least get me partial custody of Boo, which I can then use the dangle in front of my former wife to get her to come back to me.

The only problem is I know Linda's sister will fight me on it. What else am I missing that could make a judge give the sister custody over me?

– Even More Parentally Perturbed Man in Modesto

Dear Perturbed,

Shockingly, your plan has the potential to work, depending on the quality of the audio file you produced for the deathbed declaration. However, if you are not there when she dies or someone else is with you, the whole plan falls apart. If the quality of the file is not good and her sister hires an expert to dispute the recording, you will also lose. Buy some editing software to get rid of any traces of splicing, then make sure it is good enough to fool a court and hope the sister doesn't think to hire an expert.

It also falls apart if the former public defender tells the truth, but even a bad lawyer – which may well be redundant – can find employment. For him to lie about something like this and later recant would have him disbarred, so it is unlikely that he will come clean and trip you up.

Courts in situations where custody is in dispute will take into account things like family bonds and relations. However, they judge the fitness of each parental candidate as well.

You can portray yourself as a man who has dedicated his life to helping the terminally ill and play on the heartstrings of the court by saying you are the only father figure that Boo has ever known. Also, you need to start laying the groundwork to show that the sister is unfit to be a parent. Pump Linda for information on her sibling that could be incriminating. Most siblings have at least a few embarrassing stories on each other. Then follow her around at a distance and try to get incriminating video. Perhaps you could leave a lifelike doll on her doorstep with a handheld radio inside. When she comes home, use the walkie-talkie to make it seem as if the infant is crying. When the sister lifts the doll up, say rude or disgusting to make her drop or throw it, perhaps whispering that the doll is now going to explode. By that point, she will have realized it is a toy and hopefully hurl it as far away as possible.

Enter video of that episode into evidence and it will grant you a better chance of being named the infant's guardian. You may not even have to go that far. You might get lucky and the sister will turn out to be a shoplifting, drunk driving, incestuous cannibal who said something politically incorrect on social media. However, if she is the only surviving blood relative, even that might not be enough for some judges to rule against her. Good luck.

Dear Cthulhu,

My baby's mama is getting to be a real pain in my rump, if you know what I mean. I've been living here with her for the last three months, ever since our little bundle of joy – and by joy I mean misery – was born. The ho and I met in a bar one night. I'll admit she's a little bit out of my league, but the fact that she was drunk and some guy slipped a rufie into her booze didn't hurt my chances. I saw the guy do it and I told him if he didn't leave the bar I'd blow the whistle. He took off for the hills, which is good because there's no reason he should benefit from such a heinous act. But since it was already done, there was no reason I shouldn't, especially since I was doing the right thing by running him off. Apparently the drug made me look hot and she was all over me.

When the ho woke up the next morning, it took me about fifteen minutes to get her to stop screaming. She didn't remember anything about the night before, so I showed her a video I took. The ho was ticked, screaming that she was a virgin and had been saving herself for marriage.

I told her it was own fault for not keeping her pants on and that she really wasn't that great in the sack and if she wanted to be better she needed to practice a lot more. I even offered to help. The ho had the nerve to threaten to call the cops. I took off, figuring I'd never see her again. Unfortunately, I left my wallet behind and she found my driver's license. Pity, because otherwise she never would have found me, even if for some reason she didn't believe my name was really James Bond.

I got a call from her a few months later, saying that she was pregnant. I told her there's no way that baby was mine. She said I was the only guy she ever did it with, which was a crock far as I was concerned. I mean, I've never met a virgin over fourteen. I told her she couldn't fool me – I watched talk shows and wanted to go on one to get a paternity test.

We went. Unfortunately, the paternity test showed that I was indeed the baby's daddy. This particular ho believes in family values and that kinda crap. She thinks that every baby should have a mommy and daddy. She even offered to marry me. Apparently, in her religion, it's a big deal if parents aren't married. I told her no way, that I wasn't gonna be tied down.

Then I told her she would have to pay me for child support and took her to court. Using a recording of the show, the court took money out of my welfare check to pay her child support. That's what I get for doing a good deed and helping her out in the bar that night. I shoulda let her go home with the guy who rufied her. That would've taught the ho a lesson.

The ho offered to let me move in with her so I could help her raise the baby. I figured free rent and free nookie was a deal I couldn't pass up. Turns out she's making me sleep in the guest bedroom, so there ain't no hanky or even panky going on. She breastfeeds right in front of me, which makes me nuts because her knockers got so freaking huge. The ho won't let me near them, but she lets the baby. I told her she shouldn't be showing her boobs to no infant and I was going to call the cops and report her as a child molester if she didn't let me have a go at them. She didn't, so I called 911. They laughed and hung up.

After that, she says I need to carry my weight. She wants me to do chores like wash the dishes, clean the house, and have dinner ready when she gets home. And she had the nerve to say I wasn't doing a good job watching the brat. Every morning after she leaves for work, I put him in his crib, throw in a couple of bottles then duct tape some cardboard over the top so he can't get out. The brat cries all day long, but do I complain? No, I do not. I just turn up the volume on the TV to drown it out like any good dad would.

Then this ho has the nerve to accuse me of not changing his diaper all day. I tell her that all that poop and pee happens right before she gets home. Might be true even since I never check. What would be the point? I ain't touching no dirty, stinky diaper. It's enough that I remember to take the cardboard and duct tape off before she gets home so she don't have to do it.

The ho's given me a week to shape up or ship out. I don't think it's fair. In fact, I think she should pay me for providing day care. Can I sue her for alimony and child support? Maybe back pay for being her daycare worker? Can I get a judge to make her do all the chores that interrupted my day with all this nonsense? Or fake an injury and make her pay me for worker's comp?

– Proud Pappy in Peekskill

Dear Proud,

In nature, many animals eat their young. In your case, I think the reverse would be justified as you took advance of a drugged female to procreate. Sadly, human babies have neither the teeth nor jaw strength to make that practical.

In order to get alimony, you first have to be married. And in order to get child support you have to be the one taking care of the child. Since you are not wed and what you are doing with your offspring sounds more like neglect and abuse, you qualify for neither. No reasonable judge will make the child's mother do those chores and since you are the child's biological father, not only are you not an employee but you have an obligation to take care of your offspring.

Your options are simple. Do what your child's mother requests or move out. I recommend the latter because it sounds like they would both be better off without you in their lives.

Dear Cthulhu,

I'm five years old and I got a kitten for Christmas. It was the most wonderful little cat in the world. He would play with string and let me pet him all day long. I named him Buttons. One day a month ago, Buttons got out and we couldn't find him. It was a white, wintery day and my family had been making a snowman and we didn't see where Buttons went. We looked for weeks, even put up flyers and signs, but no Buttons. Then we got a warm day and the snow melted. We found Buttons dead on the lawn. We had a funeral and buried him. After the funeral, my big sister whispered in my ear that the snowman we made had come to life and eaten Buttons, then pooped him out onto the lawn underneath the snow. I think she's making it up, especially since all the snowmen on the Christmas specials are happy, friendly, and don't eat pets.

I've been having nightmares about snowman chasing me and trying to eat me as a herd of cats run by. They all have Buttons's face. I need to know the truth. Can snowman come alive and eat cats? Or kids? The weatherman is saying we're supposed to get a big blizzard this weekend. My parents are already talking about making another snowman. I need to know whether or not I have to stop them.

Thank you.

– Five Years Old and Missing Buttons.

Dear Missing,

Most snowmen do not even have a chance of doing anything but melting. For a snowman to come to life, it requires dark magic far beyond what the average human could manage. However, there could be an evil sorcerer or witch in your neighborhood that is going around and bringing snowmen to life. And if that is the case, you are lucky all it ate was a kitten. One evil snowman broke into a family's house and devoured them all. He almost got away with it too but made the mistake of crossing in front of the fireplace and melted. All the police found was a carrot and two eyes made out of coal.

I checked the weather report for your area and they are saying it is going to be good packing snow. I suggest putting the heat in your house up to ninety degrees and sleeping with an acetylene torch instead of a Teddy bear just in case.

Oh, and don't go outside until at least springtime.

Dear Cthulhu,

It's me again, NecroPhil. I dug up my dead wife, checked for the nipple ring to make sure I had the right corpse and had sex with her three times to apologize for sleeping with her dead sister. The problem is, it's just wasn't the same. It wasn't as good. Her sister's corpse is much better than my wife's is. I didn't like the way Gemini was looking at me. I think she knew what happened and was giving me the evil eye. Her sister Gemina, on the other hand, seems to have a permanent smile on her face. I like to think our time together may be the reason why. Or maybe the undertaker did something to her face.

I'm thinking of going back to the cemetery and taking one of the bodies home with me, so I can have sex whenever I want to without any of the drawbacks of a relationship like having to listen to her yap about her day or wearing a condom. I have a large chest freezer in the garage and figure I can keep the body there. The question is who should it be? My wife, with whom I had 10 years of bliss or her dead sister who apparently is a much better corpse lover?

– NecroPhil

Dear NecroPhil,

Cthulhu can see from my inbox that you have emailed Cthulhu forty-seven more times and you are boring me, so this will be my last response to you. If mating with a corpse makes you happy, then do it and choose the one that gives you the most pleasure.

However, be aware that you are racking up a list of felonies from desecrating a corpse to grave robbing to storing of human remains without the proper licenses. You must think about what will happen if somebody goes into your garage to get a hamburger or some ice cream and sees a corpse there. The reaction will likely not be a good one. And if the person who sees the corpse, or worse, catches you in the act, happens to be your brother-in-law you will have to do a lot more than explain yourself. Especially if he checks for body piercings. Although a way around this would be to switch the piercing to the other side. At least that way you can pass the corpse off as your bride rather than his.

Since you have ignored my advice about trying to procreate with a living partner, you likely will ignore the rest of it as well, but your activities will have less chance of getting caught if you change residences to somewhere with a lot of property, maybe out in the woods. And make sure you relocate the freezer personally instead of having the movers do it.

Dear Cthulhu,

I have a fairly unique hobby which might be considered a trifle ghoulish – I dig up graves.

I don't do it for money or jewelry, although I'm not opposed to taking those. I do it because I'm into costuming and there is a cemetery near my house that has graves from before the Revolutionary War up to the 1960's when they ran out of room. It's a treasure trove of period clothing.

I'll be the first to admit that some of the clothes that I take off the corpses – or in some cases bones – are not in the best condition. There can be tears and holes in the outfits. Plus, there is a certain stink to the clothes. I tried washing them at first, but it just as often destroyed as cleaned them, so I learned how to do my own dry-cleaning. That helps. Still, it doesn't always get rid of the odor.

And to be honest, it's my dad's fault I got into this stuff. He does these Revolutionary and Civil War reenactments and he forces me go with him. Because I'm a girl, the stupid rules say I can't dress as a soldier and have to be support staff. There's only so many times I can play a nurse without getting bored.

I came up with an angle that enabled me to use the clothes without making too many repairs. I stole a page from the trend where they take a classic book and add a few paragraphs about zombies and get a bestseller. I learned how to do some makeup and started going as a zombie in period clothes. The zombie thing makes it more fun, especially since I pretend to eat the brains of the fallen soldiers who aren't allowed to move thanks to those same stupid rules.

Well, to make a long story short, the local newspaper and TV stations that were sent to cover the event picked up on what I was doing and put me on TV and in the paper. My dad and the other reenactors were mad at first until they got like a hundred more people coming to their events. I've become a local celebrity. Now the other kids who get dragged to these things by their dads are being nice to me and asking me if I would make them costumes and help them with zombie makeup. I was thrilled, to say the least, so I said sure. It wasn't until later that I realized how much digging I would have to do, not to mention dragging the old wooden coffins out of the holes, putting them back in, stripping the corpse and filling in the graves back in.

Now I don't want to give you the wrong idea. I don't leave the corpses without any clothes. In fact, I give them a bit of a makeover, using modern outfits I get from our local Salvation Navy store. Mostly I use sweatpants and novelty T-shirts. My personal favorite was the one that said, *Today is the first day of the rest of your life.* My second favorite was one I used when I found a mother and child who were put in a coffin together. I've put an *I'm with stupid* T-shirt on the kid so the arrow was pointed at her mother. I figure the kid would have gotten a kick out of it.

My question is this – do you think I could ask the other reenactment kids to help me out? It would save me a lot of work and maybe give us something to bond over. I don't have a lot of friends and figure this could be a good opportunity for me. To be honest, most of them didn't want anything to do with me until they figured out they might be able to get on TV at the next reenactment, but I think I can win them over.

Obviously, this is something I couldn't talk to my father about, so I hope you'll help me.

–Grave Robbing Fashionista in Fairfield

Dear Fairfield,

Cthulhu finds a good guideline to follow when trying to gauge the trustworthiness of a human being is simply this – do not trust anyone. Given the right opportunity, persuasion, or the tiniest bit of torture, the majority of humanity will sell out their fellow humans inside of five minutes. Less if it involves the opportunity to get on television. In all likelihood, if these other children found out where you got the clothes they would tell both their parents and the same news people in order to get the spotlight shifted onto them and get their 15 minutes of fame.

Cthulhu will concede the possibility that out of a sizable number, one or two might be willing to assist you in your grave robbing, but it is not worth the risk. Grave robbing is still a crime that is on the books in many jurisdictions. It would likely go on your permanent record and affect your ability to get into a good college or trade school. Although failing that, you could always get a job as a grave digger, although they have updated their techniques so you best make sure you are well-versed in the use of a backhoe.

Dear Cthulhu,

My Mom is obsessed with weight, hers and anybody else's. If she talked about any other group of people like she does fat people, folks would call her a racist or a bigot. It all stems back to somebody once calling her fat in sixth grade and making her cry. Instead of getting over it or calling them a name back, she dedicated her life to never been called fat again.

She got a job as a personal trainer, so she can work out 8 to 10 hours a day with her clients. Mom takes my BMI every day and has since I was in diapers. It's a way to measure the percentage of body fat. One day I was 20%, over her personal allowable maximum of 18% for anyone who lived in her house and suddenly all good food was taken away from me. I have to eat Brussels sprouts and wheat germ. If I'm lucky I get some tofu. Mom puts a bunch of vegetables in a juicer and makes me drink the sludge. It's terrible.

I'm in fifth grade and I used to get to buy lunch in school. Only now, some lady in Washington DC said school lunches are bad so Mom won't let me eat them anymore. Now I have to go with a packed lunch. Bean sprouts on a wafer thin rice cracker isn't enough to sustain a fish let alone a growing kid.

We have a bully at school who goes around stealing kids' lunches. We were friends back in second grade, so, for the most part, he left me alone until the fourth day of my Mom's health food diet. He grabbed my collar in the lunch room and demanded I give him my lunch. I would've gladly, except the lack of food made me cranky and a little crazy. I turned around, grabbed and threw him on the ground, then sat on top of him and demanded he give me his lunch. This is really impressive when you consider he was left back twice and was almost as big as the teachers.

He forked the goods over and I ate well for the first time in a week. PB&J never tasted so good. The problem was the next day came and I was back to eating food a rabbit wouldn't touch, so I went after the bully for his lunch again. I figured turnabout is fair play. Things were good for a couple of weeks. Then one day he was absent. Since lunch was the only decent meal I got, I snapped a little inside and turned on the other kids. I tried not to be mean and asked for a half a sandwich here, a cookie there. I got to the point where I was getting a little something from everybody and loving it.

After a week of that, my body fat index shot up another percent and my Mom freaked, insisting she had to take me to an endocrinologist.

To top it all off, one of the kids squealed to their parents on me. Now Mom is coming to school for a conference and the teachers are watching me, so I'm not going be able to get any more lunches. Turns out the rat was the bully. I thought he would've had more class.

I think I may end up starving to death. What can I do?

– Boy in Mahwah Forced to Survive on What Rabbits Throw Away

Dear Boy,

Your government has mandated certain requirements for children's nutrition. At the conference, simply tell the principal how your mother has been treating you, what she is feeding you for your meals and that you feel like you are starving. He will likely have a talk with your mother about getting some more appropriate food for someone your age. If that doesn't change things, continue to tell him and he may call children's protective services, which will then try and force your mother into feeding you something different. If that does not work, they will take you away to live in a foster home with people who don't love you, but will lose their monthly check if they don't feed you, so at least you will get to eat.

Dear Cthulhu,

My Dad served for 20 years in the Marine Corps. Because of this service, he got a great deal of respect from others. Sadly, he died a few years back, but he'd be rolling over in his grave if he knew what his son, my brother "Joe", was doing.

Joe's always been a bit of a wayward soul. We traveled all over the world with Dad growing up, so we never really had much of a stable home environment and Joe didn't make friends easily. It only got worse when he got kicked out of Clown College. For a time, he was actually living on the streets, but I let him come sleep on my couch. During the time he was homeless, Joe started taking clothes from charities and apparently someone had donated an Army soldier's uniform. It was his size and durable so he started wearing it around. He wasn't panhandling for money, but he found out that when he was wearing the uniform people would come up to him to thank him for his service. Sometimes they would give him things. Most of the time it was a couple bucks, but sometimes it was more. One generous soul even gave him a used car. Another one offered him a job.

The problem is he continues to cut his hair and dress like he's in the military. Now that he's not homeless and looks – and smells – more respectable sometimes people just come up to him to thank him for his service and he has the gall to tell them "You're welcome". He tends to go out to eat at diners in full Army uniform because a great deal of the time people will actually pay for his meal to thank him for his service.

I've talked to him about this over and over, but he tells me that it's none of my business and that he's not going to stop.

I so want to expose him, but he'll lose his job and he's almost got enough saved for his first and last month's rent on his own apartment. He's even getting a small discount on that because his landlord's a vet. I'm thinking about threatening to expose him anyway unless he actually enlists and does at least two years of service. I figure it'll do him some good and when he gets out at least he won't be lying anymore.

Do you think it'll work? Or do you have a better idea?

– Sister of an Imitation Soldier near Fort Brag

Dear Sister,

Even Cthulhu finds this type of behavior appalling. Humans do not have many positive attributes, but the willingness of the soldier lay down his life to protect his country is an admirable one, even if Cthulhu can't imagine anything more important than me that would be worth getting a tentacle sprain for, let alone dying to save. For your brother to lay claim to military service falsely is a despicable act.

You can try to blackmail him, but it has been Cthulhu's experience with the type of humans who lie about their accomplishments to elicit praise and personal gain that just a threat will not faze him. It certainly will not be enough to make him enlist. He could have done this already if that was his true desire, but he prefers the lie.

Cthulhu has two possible solutions. Your brother does not sound exactly like the sharpest chainsaw in the shed, so type up a piece of paper and mail it to your house, stating that Joe has been drafted. State the need for secrecy and that national security forbids him from speaking of it to anyone. Outline that he must go down to his nearest recruiting station and sign up for a two-year stint in the military. And that if he does not, he will be put into prison for desertion. Mention that they have heard him bragging about his service, yet they can find no evidence of said service and that is a crime. However, the government will forgive him after this stint of service.

If that does not work, find out when and where the nearest event honoring soldiers in your area is. Tell him that someone called and invited him. Then tell the other soldiers what he is doing. They will likely make sure he never pretends to be a soldier again.

Dear Cthulhu,

In some circles, I would be considered a genius. Unfortunately, it took me years to find out where those circles were hiding.

I made my first kill I was 16. He was one of my school mates and I did it because I wanted to date his girlfriend. Every time I asked her out she told me she already had a boyfriend, so I took care of that. Turns out that she just been stringing me along, since I asked her out the next time I saw her and she said that I was insensitive, just because I asked her on a date during her boyfriend's wake.

So I waited a couple weeks and offed her too, only this time I kept the body. She was such a pretty thing that I couldn't bear to not have her with me. I experimented a little bit with carving up a corpse and learned a lot about the inner workings of the human body, both from books at the library and the Internet.

Luckily, I have a large trust fund and I was able to indulge my habit, killing people and then cutting up the remains. After a while, I got the idea to try to make the bodies into works of art.

I did a pretty good job if I do say so myself. Then I saw in the paper how this one group was taking a bunch of cut up cadavers on tour around the country. I bought a ticket and went. To be honest, they did ice work, but it was nothing compared to mine.

I forged documents that made it look like people donated their bodies to me, using fake names for each of them. I changed the faces into various shapes so that loved ones couldn't recognize them and I went on tour. It was a hit. I was making so much money I didn't even need my trust fund anymore. Even better, art critics were calling me a genius.

What's the problem, you ask? I know, it sounds like I was living the dream. Killing at will and flaunting the bodies as trophies in front of everybody. The problem is that I made such an impact that one old woman actually went and willed me her body.

I don't want it. There's nothing aesthetically pleasing about her form. What's more, I don't feel connected to the corpse having not been the one to kill it. The thing is, I'm worried that if I don't accept and do something with it that I'll raise suspicion.

Will I be selling out my art if I try and make a display out of this old woman's body? The last thing I want to be is a sellout.

– Artful Killer in Albany

Dear Artful,

First off, Cthulhu would like to again state his viewpoint regarding human on human killing - Cthulhu is against it. Humans are my property and future subjects and no one else should destroy my property without my express permission. That being said, Cthulhu looked at the pictures of your work that you sent with your letter. Very dark, disturbing, yet beautiful. I must commend you. Few humans have your talent. Fewer still would've thought to use such a unique canvas.

As for whether or not using about using the donated corpse that you did not kill would be selling out, I have to admit that I never understood the term well. As I comprehend it is usually stated by people who are less successful towards people who have made money doing something that they enjoy. Sometimes it has been done by compromising, but is it not it better to compromise and make a living at something you love than to hold on to your principles and end up having to do something else to put food on the table and a roof over your head? And in your case, having actual donated bodies in your traveling art show would be a very good thing indeed. If anyone ever came looking you would have solid proof of where those bodies came from and it would throw suspicion away from you, allowing you to do what you love even longer. In fact, on this one and any other donated corpses, you could leave the face so it could be seen so people do not wonder why you have never done it before. In fact, you should probably make a token effort in your literature and website to solicit donations from people who die. And if you ever have parts left over from a fresh kill, particularly inner organs, please put them in dry ice and ship them to me. They make for tasty snacks.

Dear Cthulhu,

I have a problem. My big sister is obsessed with the eighties. I don't mean the decade. I mean, she's obsessed with men in their eighties.

A while back, she got in trouble with the law for selling pirate DVDs. I don't mean she pirated movies. She snuck up to our neighbor's window and filmed him dancing around naked with a parrot. Well, he wasn't exactly naked. He had a hat with a skull and crossbones, an eye patch and a hook. She made videos of him singing it's a *Pirate's Life for Me, Sixteen Men on a Dead Man's Chest* and, oddly enough, *All the Single Ladies*. I have to admit watching this man shiver his timber was amusing, but I think she crossed the line by actually selling DVDs to people. The police agreed and got her under some Peeping Tom law. She got sentenced to five hundred hours of community service and started working in a nursing home near our house.

At first, it seemed like a good thing. "Britney" had always been a bit of a self-centered twit. I can say that because I'm her sister and we have to share a room. She never really cared about anybody else but herself. Working in the nursing home seemed to change that. In the beginning she was annoyed, but then she seemed to look forward to it. Britney said she was going to keep on volunteering even after she served her time. She even dumped her loser boyfriend, which made Mom and Dad very happy. I mean, she was a senior and eighteen years old. It was about time she started shaping up.

Then one Saturday she came home, beaten and bruised. I wanted to take her to the hospital, but she refused. She didn't want Mom and Dad to know. I had to do her makeup to hide a bruise on her face. She was hurting so bad, we stole one of Dad's Vicodin and gave it to her. While she was loopy from the drug, she told me what actually happened. Turns out for all the months she's been volunteering at the nursing home, she's actually been sleeping with the older men. Not just one or two, but every guy in the nursing home over the age of 80, including one in a coma, although she swears for the time she was with him, he wasn't comatose, or at least part of him wasn't.

The old geezers apparently really enjoy her company, so they've all kept their traps shut and don't seem to mind sharing her. She had a couple close calls, like with one guy who dislocated his total hip while they were getting busy. She thought another guy died, but then his pacemaker kicked in and brought him back.

What happened that Saturday was she was having her way with a guy who was 89 years old. She claims they were going at it hard – she says wrinkles turn her on. Ick. The thought of it makes me want to barf. They forgot to lock the room door and the guy's wife came to visit. Apparently, he liked his women younger as she was only 73. Upon finding Britney riding her hubby who looks like a wrinkled manatee, she proceeded to beat the crap out of her with a cane. Sis says she barely made it out of there alive and with her clothes. The old woman almost caught her, but one of her other lovers stuck his walker out and tripped the old biddy.

Sis is worried that the old woman is gonna squeal on her. She's only got twenty-five more hours to serve out her sentence, but she's afraid to go back. She says she figures what she did is legal and okay because she's 18. I don't because I think it's disgusting.

She's begging me not to tell Mom. So far, I can't figure out a way to tell my mother that her daughter is dating a man old enough to be my Mom's grandfather. Or rather, a group of men who collectively are probably over a thousand.

Even worse, she asked one of the codgers to prom. She says he barely looks a day over seventy-five and he's willing to spring for a corsage, a limo, a bottle of Viagra and a case of condoms. I think it would be social suicide. I pointed out that everyone will talk about it in our town so much that she'll have trouble getting a job when she graduates. Or worse – she might kill one of them.

That didn't bother her too much. Sis told me that all the old guys said that they put her in their wills. She figured if they went, she'd get a big payout. I told her that was doubtful at best unless she saw it in writing. I'm only sixteen, but even I know that a guy will tell you anything to get into your pants. I doubt that changes just because he gets elderly. In fact, since the old and wrinkly are less likely to get any, they'd make their lies even bigger.

Britney wants me to tell her what she should do and I just don't know. Do you think the old woman squealed on her? Should she go back and try to get those last few hours in any way? Should I tell my parents? And how do I talk her out of taking a guy with more wrinkles than a Shar-Pei to one of the most important social events of her life?

-Little Sister of a Grandpa Chaser in Roanoke

Dear Roanoke,

Your sister is correct when she says it is legal. If she was under 18, the old men in question could be charged with statutory rape. Even though she's in high school, she is considered a legal adult and can make her own decisions, no matter how poor or warped they might seem to others.

Cthulhu endorses your take on the male of your species. Men as a whole will lie to the female of the species for even an outside chance at procreation. Although it sounds like your sister is more of a sure thing.

A woman scorned is capable of almost anything. Your sister should probably contact someone she trusts at the nursing home to see if the wife reported her yet. If she has, she should finish her hours elsewhere as they will likely ban her. If they press the issue, she can claim sexual harassment and threaten to sue. She can tell the men to back up her story if they ever want to procreate with her again.

If the old woman hasn't reported it, your sister should offer to make her a deal – if the wife keeps her mouth shut, your sister will stay away from her husband and not press assault charges against her. Then she should quickly finish her remaining hours on her sentence, being careful to avoid her recreational procreation partners, especially those who already have mates.

Assuming the men were actually telling the truth about their wills, there is also a problem with being written into a will for sexual favors. The family or heirs can use that information to tie up the money in court for years, so it could be a very long time before she sees any payout.

As for the prom, Cthulhu agrees it is likely a poor social choice to attend with somebody more than four times her age. Her peers will likely not understand and taunt her over it. In the age of social media, she can be assured that pictures and video of her and her aged paramour will be posted online. However, depending on how outrageous, disgusting or promiscuous her behavior at the prom or on the dance floor is, there is always the chance that it could go viral. You mention your sister getting a job after high school, but made no mention of trade school or college, so she is headed for a menial job. Such exposure on the Internet could lead her to a sort of notoriety which might be parlayed into her so-called fifteen minutes of fame. She might become a spokeswoman for erectile dysfunction products or get a chance at a reality show. There is likely some network willing to air a show that starts out with a teen dating thirty old men and ends with one of them getting to date or marry your sister. If she decides to try each of them out in the bedroom, they should have EMTs standing by. If someone is overwhelmed by her procreation skills, it could be ratings gold.

At the very least, she could set up a website or dating profile listing her preference for old men. She will likely have no shortage of suitors. Instead of assuming she will be put into their will, she could ask for gifts in advance. This way she handles her perversion and provides for herself at the same time. I could also put her in touch with a seventy-six-year-old virgin who is extremely gullible and believes in imaginary diseases like beaver pox. Having more experience than her partner might make for an interesting change for her.

Dear Cthulhu,

I am a snake lover. I have a 12-foot boa constrictor that I've raised from when it was a tiny baby snakelet until now.

Although I have good taste in reptiles, I have poor taste in men. I'd been dating "Dutch" for the last three and a half years. For the last three, he'd been abusing me. I know I should have left him, but in all honesty, I don't have much self-esteem and sometimes he would go months without hitting me. Then Dutch would have a bad day at work or at the track, then he'd come home and take his frustrations out on me with his fists. I would have left long ago, but after we first got together he insisted I stop working so now I have no money to use to get away.

Last month he lost his entire paycheck betting on a greyhound that chased a bird instead of the mechanical rabbit on the track. When he came home he was furious, but I had one of my girlfriends over so he went into the kitchen to drink heavily and cut up some steaks to put on the grill. When my girlfriend left, I went into the basement where we keep "Bo". I was going to take him out of his cage and pet him, but no sooner had I opened the door then I felt a fist hit me in the back of my neck. I fell to the ground. All the other times Dutch beat me I knew it was coming, but this time, it caught me unaware.

Instead of being scared, I got angry. My boyfriend was on a softball team and there was a bat near where I fell. I picked it up and swung it without even looking. I nailed him right across the forehead. It didn't knock Dutch out, but it knocked him down. He was stunned and unable to get up. Bo slithered out of his cage and wrapped himself around my boyfriend, then slowly crushed his rib cage and suffocated him to death.

I admit I could have stopped it, but I didn't want to. All the beatings over the years came back to me in a rush and I enjoyed watching the bastard suffer and turn blue. The best part was him waking up. In between gasping for air, Dutch begged me to help him. Each time he spoke, he had to exhale air and let Bo tighten his coils until he couldn't get enough air to speak at all.

I just smiled and watched it all.

Once I was sure Dutch was dead, I went upstairs and called 911. The police came and found his body with Bo still wrapped around him. They were going to shoot him then and there, but I told them I could get Bo unwound. I did it and they had an animal control officer put Bo in a cage. They questioned me and I left out the part about me hitting Dutch with the baseball bat. They blamed the wound on him falling down. Luckily he'd been drinking.

In my heart, I know Bo did it to protect me, although the detective thought it was because my boyfriend had been cutting up raw meat and there was blood still on his hands. He said the snake smelled it and thought Dutch was food.

Once the cops were done questioning me, I snuck outside and managed to steal Bo from the animal control officer's truck. That snake was a hero. There was no way I was letting them take him. I hid him in an empty garbage can until after the cops left. They didn't realize the snake was missing until they got the truck to the pound. They even apologized to me for losing him and caused a minor frenzy on the evening news when it leaked out that a killer snake was loose in the community. When I asked them to reimburse me for the snake, they said they couldn't and that Bo would've been put down anyway. Also, they did some research. They told me that it's apparently a bad idea to keep a boa constrictor over ten feet long as a pet as they are big enough to kill humans.

Here's my dilemma. I don't want to get rid of Bo. I'm thinking of telling the police that I bought another snake to help me get over the loss. Also, Bo helped me make my living before I looked up with my dead boyfriend. I worked as an exotic dancer. It's sort of the same thing as a stripper, except I had a gimmick. I danced with Bo wrapped around my naughty bits. For some reason, it's a real turn-on for some guys. I was even in an indie rock video wearing a bikini and Bo way back when.

I'm going to have to pay for rent, food, and utilities soon.

Dancing is the only way I know how to make money. Do you think it's a bad idea to use Bo? Could the cops be able to identify him? As far as I know, all the pictures of me and Bo back in the day that hung in the strip joints I worked were thrown out. Even if they weren't, Bo was about a foot and a half shorter then.

Should I go back to dancing? Or do you have a better idea of how I can make a living? Also, back when I was a dancer a lot of guys hit on me and I had a tendency to be a little bit too easy. The truth is my ex-boyfriend was a dirt bag, but we had sex all the time. It was pretty okay too. I'm worried I'll do the first guy who asks and be back in the same boat. I can't expect Bo to kill all my boyfriend for me, can I?

-My Boa Bo Killed My Beau In Beaufort.

Dear Beaufort,

I think it would be a foolish proposition to expect a pet to kill your boyfriends, besides which Cthulhu is against humans killing humans, even by proxy. One day all humanity will belong to Cthulhu, so humans will be my property. I cannot condone anyone harming my livestock and future food supply. Also, if you have two boyfriends who died by snake, the police will become suspicious and probably charge you for the crime, claiming you used the snake as a weapon. Plus, the next time they will take extra precautions and you will not be able to steal your boa constrictor back.

The police may become suspicious about the snake, so it would be best if you were able to provide some sort of paper trail to show that you acquired a second snake. Perhaps you can go to a pet store and see if they would be willing to forge the documents for you. That or contact a pet rescue organization. Humans who dedicate their lives to helping lesser animals often have a twisted view of the world and forgo using their common sense in favor of overly sentimental attachments to life forms even lower than humans. More than one group has objected to Cthulhu eating kittens – with or without hollandaise sauce – if you can believe it. One of these wackadoos would undoubtedly be willing to lie and claim the snake was a rescue, rather than risk it being killed by the authorities.

As for whether or not you should return to the workforce, Cthulhu will tell you that it is far better than expecting someone else to support you, whether it be another male or your government. Could you get a job working with reptiles at a zoo or game farm? If not and you do not possess any other job skills, then you should use what you have and do what you know. Many human males are quite willing to trade money for a chance to look at the flesh of the female of the species, so if you are attractive you will likely do well. Cthulhu recommends you find ways to build your self-confidence and forgo procreation for an extended period until you can develop a sense of self-worth. Try to find someone who actually cares about you as an individual, rather than a procreational object. Otherwise, you will likely end up back in a similar situation. No one, except Cthulhu, has the right to harm you without your permission. Learn to stand up for yourself and walk away from anyone who would harm you, except of course Cthulhu. In that situation, most choose to run but they rarely get far.

Dear Cthulhu,

My son is very bright for his age and generally very well behaved. Our problem is that at the age of five he developed an absolute terror of thunderstorms. When it rains and thunders, he runs into my bed and hides under the covers, whimpering and crying.

I sympathize with him, but it's a real problem, especially in my line of work. I'm a prostitute. Now I could give you a sad story about how I was abused, came from a broken home and was molested as a child, but none of those things are true. I'm just too lazy to go out and get a regular job. I advertised on Greg's List, got a few regulars and now I don't have any problem paying the bills. I entertain men in my bedroom almost every night. It had never been a problem before because my son was a very sound sleeper and my husband works nights. However, my kid's thunderstorm behavior is really cutting into my workspace. Sometimes, when the men are banging me into the headboard, he thinks it's thunder too. Guys always make like all they want is sex – quick, down and dirty, but most of them stop and can't finish just because a crying boy climbs into bed and hides under the covers that they are humping beneath.

I tried to fix the problem myself in the traditional way, by telling him that thunder is just God bowling. It worked for about a night. Then he began to assign different pin counts to the different types of thunderclaps and he printed a bowling score sheet off our computer. He started keeping track of God's bowling scores. Worse, after each frame, he would throw open the door to my bedroom and tell me "God got a strike." Or "God got a 7 to 10 split." And apparently for most men, having someone throw open the door and shout into a room where they're paying to have sex with somebody else's wife makes them jump under the bed or out the window.

We're a churchgoing family. I know that seems odd given what I do, but the minister was one of my first customers and I picked up a lot of work among the congregation. It's fairly easy to tell which women don't give their men enough attention. The problem is, my boy keeps asking people if God can do anything, then why does he has such trouble bowling a 300 game. It seems like I traded a phobia for an obsession.

He watches bowling shows and tournaments and made notes of the techniques. In his prayers, before he goes to bed he gives God bowling advice. Then he started telling the minister to please pass his bowling tips on to God because he didn't seem to be listening to him.

It turns out that the minister and three of the other members of the congregation are in a bowling league and they weren't doing too good, so they brought my son along as their coach. They've been winning almost every game and they're going to be in whatever they call the bowling playoffs. If they win that they'll be in the state championship bowl-off.

The problem is, now there are games almost every weeknight. My husband is taking off from work to go see what his son has helped do and he expects me to go. It's really cutting into my work time. On the plus side, the entire bowling team are my clients, but the people are starting to get suspicious about me spending all night in the men's room. The last thing I need is for my husband to figure things out.

I want to help my son and not lose money or my husband. Cthulhu, I need your help. What should I do?

– Working Mother in Wichita.

Dear Working,

Where shall we begin? Should Cthulhu draw attention to the fact that by prostituting yourself, you are in fact in violation of your wedding vows? And that by paying more time with – and attention to – your customers than your offspring, you are doing what may be long-term psychological harm to the boy. Cthulhu could point out that if you are making enough money from your business venture, then you could rent a room somewhere else and hire a babysitter. That or have the boy sleep with noise canceling headphones.

You might also consider charging the bowling team for your boy's coaching talents. If he really is that good, offer his services to professional bowlers who might be able to pay more in order to replace your lost income.

However, the simplest solution to having a son constantly walking in on you while you procreate for money would be to buy a lock for your bedroom door.

Have A Dark Day.

PATRICK THOMAS is the author of more than 30 books and over 150 short stories. Among his works is the fantasy humor Murphy's Lore series, which includes *Tales From Bulfinche's Pub, Fools' Day, Through The Drinking Glass, Shadow Of The Wolf, Redemption Road, Bartender Of The Gods, Nightcaps* and *Empty Graves* — as well as the After Hours spin-offs *Startenders, Constellation Prize, Fairy With A Gun, Fairy Rides The Lightning, Dead To Rites, Rites of Passage,* and *Lore & Dysorder.*

His Mystic Investigators paranormal mystery series includes *Bullets & Brimstone, From The Shadows* and *Once More Upon A Time. Assassin's Ball* is his first mystery, co-written with John French. He co-edited *New Blood* and *Hear Them Roar* and was an editor for the magazines *Fantastic Stories of the Imagination* and *Pirate Writings.*

Patrick's humorous advice column Dear Cthulhu has been running since 2005 and includes the collections *Have A Dark Day, Good Advice For Bad People, Cthulhu Knows Best* and *What Would Cthulhu Do?*

His short stories have been featured in over fifty anthologies and more than three dozen print magazines.

A number of his books were part of the props department of the CSI television show and have been spotted on the program. His urban fantasy Fairy With A Gun was optioned for film and TV by Laurence Fishburne's Cinema Gypsy Productions. Top Men Productions is developing his Soul For Hire Story, *Act of Contrition,* into a short film.

Please drop by www.patthomas.net to learn more.

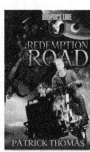

No One Is Above The Lore...
Even In Hell

Hell's Detective™

"Gritty, snappy, very dark
and very funny."
-J. L. Comeau,
Creature Feature

"Dark... and charming."
- Ellen Datow,
The Best Horror of the Year Vol.4

CPSIA information can be obtained at www.ICGtesting.com
Printed in the USA
BVOW08s1653080916

461480BV00003B/30/P